TEACHING
LEADERSHIP

Case-in-Point,
Case Studies and Coaching

CHRIS GREEN
JULIA FABRIS MCBRIDE

KLC Press
Kansas Leadership Center
325 East Douglas, Wichita, Kansas, USA, 67202

Visit our website at *www.kansasleadershipcenter.org*.

This edition published in 2015.

Library of Congress Control Number 2015941184
ISBN: 978-0-9889777-4-7

Cover and graphics designed by Clare McClaren, Novella Brandhouse
Book design by Patrick Hackenberg
Photos by Jeff Tuttle Photography

Printed in the United States of America

These other KLC Press publications are available
at *www.kansasleadershipcenter.org.*

For the Common Good: Redefining Civic Leadership
by David Chrislip and Ed O'Malley

For the Common Good: Participant Handbook
by Ed O'Malley, Julia Fabris McBride and Amy Nichols

Contact Us

The Kansas Leadership Center offers Teaching Leadership workshops
and conferences in Wichita, Kansas, and online. To register visit *www.
kansasleadershipcenter.org/teachingleadership.*

For information about customizing a training event for leadership
development professionals in your organization, email
info@kansasleadershipcenter.org.

The authors welcome your comments, questions and critiques.
Please contact Chris Green at *cgreen@kansasleadershipcenter.org.*
Contact Julia Fabris McBride at *jfmcbride@kansasleadershipcenter.org.*

This book is dedicated to:

David Chrislip
and
Ronnie Brooks

Thanks for the inspiration.

Table of Contents

Table of Contents (cont.)

Foreword

By Ed O'Malley

There are thousands and thousands of books about leadership, but few regarding how to teach it — or, more precisely, about how to create environments where it can be learned.

Maybe that's why Barbara Kellerman's critique of the leadership development field — "The End of Leadership" — is such a wake-up call for anyone who teaches leadership (or consults, facilitates, coaches, etc. about the topic), whether as a professional or volunteer. Her central argument, that with all this leadership development going on you would think we would have made more progress on the daunting challenges around us, propels questions such as:

- What exactly is leadership? Can we define it?

- If we can define it, can people learn it?

- If people can learn it, can it be taught?

- If it can be taught, how so?

This book focuses like a laser on that last question.

Kellerman's book came out in 2012. She might have enjoyed knowing our institution — the Kansas Leadership Center — has shared her hypothesis since our creation in 2007. Her book is intended to define a problem — that most leadership training doesn't seem to work — and she purposefully refrains from offering a solution.

This book and the overall work of the Kansas Leadership Center and its leadership development family is, I hope, an antidote to the problem outlined by Kellerman.

Unsatisfied with existing instruction — or lack thereof — on the topic of leadership, we set out to do something different. We wanted to crack the code on how to create provocative learning environments that result in the vast majority of learners actually becoming better at leading others. Then by extension, more progress being made on the challenges and problems facing our communities and organizations.

With resources to bear, a long view and passion to get it right, we set out with a vision to be the center of excellence for civic leadership development.

Data tell us hundreds and thousands of people who have spent time in our learning environments are more effective at making progress on tough issues. Is that 100 percent of those people? Of course not, but it's enough to feel we are on to something.

To counteract the concerns that Kellerman and KLC share, we set out in 2007 with two important objectives: first, construct a powerful yet simple framework for thinking about leadership; second, discern and develop the best ways of helping people learn that framework. This book alludes to the first objective but focuses by design on the second.

The Kansas Leadership Center exists to build the capacity of a state — all its inhabitants — to lead more effectively. A key piece of our strategy has been to increase the quantity of and quality of teachers of leadership.

But we don't simply want more teachers per se. We want more high quality teachers using proven techniques that create transformative experiences for learners. We believe leadership teaching must be much more provocative, purposeful and engaging, and this book describes methods designed with that in mind.

Julia and Chris describe our methods in this book. It's a gem for any teacher of leadership — whether a professional consultant, professor or volunteer facilitator of a community program.

Teachers of leadership, myself included, cannot simply be satisfied if we entertain and delight our audiences. We must see ourselves as attempting to mobilize others — the learners — to learn and change important things about themselves. To do so means the act of teaching leadership must be an act of leadership in and of itself. Julia and Chris paint a picture about what it looks like to exercise leadership as a teacher of leadership.

It's a fascinating picture. I hope you agree and paint yourself into it.

Ed O'Malley
President and CEO
Kansas Leadership Center

Introduction: Teaching Leadership

If you feel that something is missing in our 21st-century institutions — if you suspect that we need more and better leadership at all levels of society — and if you aspire to transform individuals and teams through education, training or coaching, then this book is for you.

In her 2010 book, "Leadership: Essential Selections on Power, Authority, and Influence," Barbara Kellerman asserts that, although there has long been consensus that leadership can be taught, "there has never been much agreement either on how leadership should be taught or on who exactly should be the leadership learner." Based on the proliferation of leadership theories in the past 20 years, she might well have added that there is little agreement on exactly what should be taught by those who desire to develop leadership capacity in others.

"Still, differences notwithstanding," Kellerman continues, "there is a common thread. By definition, the literature on learning leadership is based on the proposition that people can, and sometimes do, change. It is presumed, in other words, that we are able to learn leadership."

We agree with Kellerman that people can change and have the capacity to learn leadership. We also believe that, with coaching and support, those willing to do the work can apply what they learn about leadership to make progress on things they care about.

This book takes a stand not only about

THE LEADERSHIP LESSONS PEOPLE NEED TO LEARN, BUT ALSO ABOUT OPTIMAL WAYS TO TEACH THOSE LESSONS.

This is a textbook for KLC's *Teaching Leadership* workshops and conferences. It is designed for individuals who want to enhance their ability to develop leadership capacity in others. It is a guide for experienced practitioners who want to enhance their approach to teaching and coaching leadership.

You will not find the word "leader" in this book, except when we are referring to what others say. If you are used to associating leadership with a particular role (such as the boss or the person at the front of the room), if you believe leadership requires a certain set of characteristics (such as charisma or a thirst for the spotlight), or if you habitually use "leader" as a synonym for "person in a position of authority," we ask you to shift your thinking. We challenge you to change your approach to teaching and coaching. We encourage you to base your speech and your actions on the somewhat radical, perhaps transformational, idea of "leadership as an action."

LEADERSHIP MEANS MOBILIZING PEOPLE
TO MAKE PROGRESS ON DIFFICULT CHALLENGES.

At the root of the leadership principles, competencies and teaching methods described in this book is the following definition: "Leadership means mobilizing people to make progress on difficult challenges at work, at home and in community." The teaching methods included here are designed to support you in teaching and coaching others to take more effective action on behalf of what they care about. As you help people learn these ideas, you will empower them to exercise leadership more often and to take more risks.

Likewise, as you encourage others to practice a new approach to leadership, there will be setbacks. You will stumble. And you will be called upon to help those you work with navigate inevitable problems and conflicts.

The teaching methods contained in this book are not for those who wish to help adults become better managers or train them to solve technical problems that require skillful intervention by an expert or boss. Rather, this book (along with KLC's *Teaching Leadership* conferences and workshops) is designed to provide the background and tools you need to help people learn and practice exercising leadership on difficult and entrenched adaptive challenges (more about those challenges later).

Today's problems require a different kind of leadership. Yesterday's world view is out of date. Old frames of reference do not make sense anymore. Our companies and our communities cannot rely on a few individuals in key positions of authority to map the way forward. Instead, we need acts of leadership from countless people in all walks of life and at all levels of organizations. We need leadership that is both more purposeful and more inclusive of a wide range of voices, values and perspectives. We need patient, courageous experimenters willing to work with people with whom they disagree to create something new. We need people who are willing to step outside their own boxes, time and again, for the sake of lasting, positive change.

THIS

NEW BRAND OF LEADERSHIP

requires a different kind of leadership development, one that more adequately prepares adults for the rigors of leading in today's environments. We need leadership development that promotes

DEEP LEARNING *and* SUSTAINED GROWTH *for all.*

Each year, thousands of Kansans, plus a smattering of friends from around the globe, attend KLC programs such as *You. Lead. Now.* and *Lead for Change.* They find these experiences — some short and focused, others taking months — to be challenging and even frustrating; however, most people report that the learning leaves them better equipped for the hard work of making progress in multiple contexts.

This book and KLC's *Teaching Leadership* workshops and conferences share the teaching methods behind those experiences and offer practical guidance for using those methods to achieve your goals. We hope you will use this book to help others develop the courage and take the action to move ahead on something they care about. We hope this book inspires, instructs and provokes conversation among all those committed to mobilizing people to make progress on difficult problems in companies and communities around the world.

Leadership Principles and Competencies

If you want to teach or coach using the methods in this book, you should familiarize yourself with five leadership principles and four competencies (see Figures 1 and 2).

FIGURE I:

Leadership Principles

- Leadership is an activity, not a position.
- Anyone can lead, anytime, anywhere
- It starts with you and must engage others
- Your purpose must be clear.
- It's risky.

Leadership Competencies

DIAGNOSE SITUATION

- Explore tough interpretations
- Distinguish technical and adaptive work
- Understand the process challenges
- Test multiple interpretations and points of view
- Take the temperature
- Identify who needs to do the work

ENERGIZE OTHERS

- Engage unusual voices
- Work across factions
- Start where they are
- Speak to loss
- Inspire a collective purpose
- Create a trustworthy process

MANAGE SELF

- Know your strengths, vulnerabilities and triggers
- Know the story others tell about you
- Choose among competing values
- Get used to uncertainty and conflict
- Experiment beyond your comfort zone
- Take care of yourself

INTERVENE SKILLFULLY

- Make conscious choices
- Raise the heat
- Give the work back
- Hold to purpose
- Speak from the heart
- Act experimentally

The five principles, four competencies and 24 leadership behaviors (listed in Figures 1 and 2) form the framework of KLC's teaching, coaching and consulting. KLC's teaching methods were designed to help people learn and apply those ideas. The five principles and four competencies form a strong core around which you can frame your leadership development programs and curriculum.

These ideas were developed after a yearlong listening tour during which KLC staff talked with individuals and small groups about what makes leadership difficult and what kind of leadership it would take to achieve their aspirations. We filtered those ideas and tested them with experts from the fields of leadership, leadership development and civic engagement. From there, we outlined these leadership principles and competencies to support people who care about making progress in a variety of contexts.

It is worth noting that these principles and competencies do not cover every behavior necessary to lead successfully. They are weighted toward difficult or uncomfortable behaviors, those that take courage and practice, those skills and actions that typically don't come naturally to human beings.

Adaptive Challenges

The KLC leadership principles and competencies are based on the conception of leadership first put forward by Ron Heifetz and Donald Laurie and later expanded by Heifetz, Marty Linsky and others. In their view, leadership is the practice of mobilizing people to tackle tough adaptive challenges and thrive. Adaptive challenges are those problems or issues for which there are no clear solutions. They are different from problems, no matter how large or complex, that can be solved by bringing in the right expert or attracting the proper focus from authority. With adaptive challenges, people and groups must work together differently, often working through conflict to navigate new terrain, deal with loss, arrive at a shared purpose and generate capacity to thrive in a changing world.

Here's a simple example of how to differentiate adaptive challenges from more straightforward technical problems.

If the brakes on your car are failing, there is an easy fix. Take the car to a repair shop and hire an expert, a mechanic, who has skills and knowledge that are probably beyond your competence, certainly beyond ours. For you, the problem is beyond your capacity. For the mechanic, it is right in the wheelhouse and can be tackled with a high degree of certainty that the intervention will be successful. But let's say that your 85-year-old father has recently moved in with you. He has been driving your car and, given his failing eyesight, prefers to keep his foot on the brake all the time just in case he needs to stop quickly. Getting new brakes will only provide a temporary fix.

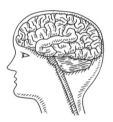

TECHNICAL PROBLEMS
LIVE IN PEOPLE'S HEADS AND LOGIC SYSTEMS.
They are susceptible to facts and authoritative expertise.

ADAPTIVE CHALLENGES
LIVE IN PEOPLE'S HEARTS AND STOMACHS.
They are about values, loyalties and beliefs.

Like most complex problems, your brake problem has elements that are technical (the brakes do not function properly) and aspects that are adaptive (your father has been driving a car for over 60 years and for him driving symbolizes his continuing to lead an independent life, an important part of his self-identity). For him to stop driving would rip part of his heart out.

Making progress on adaptive challenges requires a commitment to the five leadership principles. Progress requires engaging in all of the behaviors detailed in the KLC leadership competencies, intervening in new ways and paying constant attention to whether others are becoming more or less engaged in a shared purpose. Leadership on adaptive challenges demands the ability to manage oneself and the willingness to act experimentally, taking risks when necessary to achieve an important goal.

The Three-Legged Stool

Of course, a list of principles and competencies, no matter how researched, nuanced or accurate, will never be enough to change behavior. Old habits die hard. New skills often don't come naturally. As most teachers and coaches know, adults learn new habits and skills only through experience. They learn new leadership skills by practicing them. They learn through trial and error and through failure.

Adults need teachers equipped with methods proven to work for adults. No single approach will do. Therefore, this book contains a trio of teaching methods — a three-legged stool from atop which you can provide what adults need to understand and apply new leadership skills. Once you understand these methods and have a chance to practice them (either in a KLC *Teaching Leadership* offering or in work sessions with your colleagues), you will have what you need to help learners make progress on adaptive challenges they face.

In the chapters that follow, you will be introduced to the teaching methods of the three-legged stool and find resources to help you use them.

Of all the methods KLC could have chosen to deliver its curriculum, why did it choose these three? The answer is threefold.

First of all, each is engaging and interactive. Coaching rests on a deeply collaborative relationship between the learner and coach. When done skillfully, Case-in-Point and case teaching grab people's attention and keep it. They create the space for a wider variety of interactions to happen in a classroom. Learners can gain from each other as much as they do the teacher.

All three methods also create numerous opportunities for learners to rapidly apply the concepts they are studying. They don't have to wait for the class or coaching session to end to try it out at home. They can begin experimenting in the moment to diagnose a situation, raise the heat or explore tough interpretations. They leave an experience with more than just an intellectual understanding of leadership. They've wrestled with how to actually live it out in their lives.

The final reason is this stool provides crucial support as learners come to understand themselves in new ways. Although they tend to be more fluid than traditional methods, the teacher or coach still plays a very key role in helping the learner make sense of their experience and integrate new behaviors into their repertoire. By skillfully using their authority role, teachers and coaches can assist learners while they navigate dead-ends and bumps in the road and reassure them that they are on a path to personal growth.

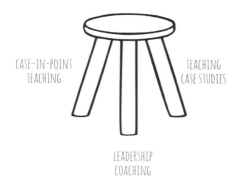

FIGURE 3:

The Three-Legged Stool

Case-in-Point Teaching

Far too often, leadership classes fall short because they are too safe, comfortable and easy. They fail to re-create in any significant way the difficult conditions in which good leadership results in real progress. They also fail to provide environments where people can actually practice the leadership behaviors they are supposed to be learning. Case-in-Point teaching, the first leg of the stool, described in Chapter 1, compels learners to practice leadership competencies in real time, in the protected space of the classroom, and in an environment resembling the real-life situations in which they want to make a difference.

We have made classroom-based Case-in-Point central to most KLC programs precisely because it creates an intensity that mimics real life. When a class uses itself as a case study for leadership, the experience can be profound. When many of us experienced it for the first time — at KLC or in another setting — we found ourselves wide awake, on the edge of our seats, fascinated with what was happening in the room around us. The experience made us feel as if we were back in the legislature, at an intense company meeting or at the school board wrestling with a budget that just wouldn't stretch to meet the competing needs of a roomful of citizens.

Teaching Case Studies

Chapter 2 is devoted to the second leg of the stool, teaching case studies, another proven method with a decades-long track record. Case studies have been used at Harvard and other universities in subjects as varied as law, business and public policy. Case studies shift focus from the instructor to learners, who wrestle with real-life challenges in stories that jump from the printed page to the center of classroom discussion. Learners apply what they are learning to the case as their teacher encourages them to consider divergent viewpoints and multiple options for action. In our context, case study teaching helps bridge the gap between the theory and practice of leadership.

To teach case studies successfully, teachers don't present information themselves. Instead, they have students read a story about a situation that requires leadership. In our programs, those stories are lifted from the accounts of Kansas civic and organizational life. Then, teachers ask powerful questions, engaging groups in vigorous discussion and debate. Skilled teachers prompt learners to direct comments to one another, not just to the teacher, making it more likely that powerful leadership lessons come from the group.

KLC has created a library of more than a dozen full-length cases, which will be available to readers of this book through online download. These in-depth stories have multiple sections and feature a number of different characters. Teachers use them to conduct discussions lasting as long as two hours or more.

Full-length cases aren't the right choice for every leadership learning opportunity. Shorter versions of the KLC case studies — called case vignettes — allow you to bring the power of cases into more settings.

Whether full-length or vignette, these cases can be used to inspire and invoke discussion about the dynamics of leadership, such as exercising leadership without authority, engaging unusual voices, using authority to lead effectively, working across factions, bringing conflict to the surface and working with competing values.

Leadership Coaching

Changing one's behavior over time is a personal experience that requires personalized support. Leadership coaching, the third leg of the stool, deepens and sustains learning in the weeks after a classroom experience. At KLC, we match learners with highly skilled, intensively trained coaches, providing a partner in early efforts to apply new skills. Coaching has become a core element at KLC because it works.

Recognizing that deep learning about leadership (the kind of learning we ask for in KLC programs) is also adaptive work, with its own risks and need for support and accountability, we added coaching as a core element. We suspected then, and our evaluation data continue to prove, that adding coaching to an intense program experience dramatically increases the likelihood that ideas presented in the classroom get translated into action in the field.

Chapter 3 provides a deep dive into KLC's individual coaching model and is a guide for coaches and program developers who are considering coaching as an intervention, either on its own or in conjunction with a classroom training experience.

Foundation Beneath the Stool

As you teach and coach, you'll need to introduce the KLC leadership competencies and principles and facilitate discussion about them. Sometimes the best way to do this is with traditional presentation and facilitation, the foundation beneath your three-legged stool (see Chapter 4).

Although this book does not attempt to instruct you on the nuts and bolts of presentation and facilitation (an excellent resource for that is "Adults Learning" by Jenny Rogers), it does provide outlines of sessions, along with suggestions for how to use them. Beginning teachers and volunteer facilitators might wish to use the outlines as written, whereas more advanced practitioners might use them in concert with a case study, in the midst of a Case-in-Point session or to underline an idea during a coaching conversation.

How to Practice and Provide Feedback

Whether you are a novice leadership developer or have been teaching, coaching or consulting for several decades, integrating new methods, such as those described in this book, will require you to practice and get feedback. Walking into a classroom without sufficient, deliberate practice does a disservice to everyone involved. At KLC, for instance, our teachers use a four-step process to prepare to deliver a session for the first time. This process is especially crucial when you are just beginning to use a teaching method such as case teaching or Case-in-Point.

Step 1

KNOW YOUR PLAN.

Identify your teaching objectives and outline the session.
Review it in your mind. Practice delivering it on your own.

Step 2

PRACTICE WITH A KNOWLEDGEABLE OBSERVER.

Rehearse at least three times in front of someone who knows
what you are aiming for and has a good idea of what mastery
of both the topic and teaching methods looks like.

Step 3

TEACH THE NEW SESSION TO ACTUAL LEARNERS.

Teach the new session to actual learners. The first time you
teach a session, invite your knowledgeable observer to attend
and provide feedback.

Step 4

**TEACH THE SESSION OR USE THE NEW
METHODOLOGY AGAIN AND AGAIN AND AGAIN.**

It is only through repeated, productive practice that we gain
expertise. Stay aware of what works and doesn't work each time
you deliver the session.

Teaching that appears effortless takes years of effort. Great teachers know their content inside and out. They are so comfortable with their delivery methods that they can deal with whatever arises. From that base of knowledge and comfort they are released to be creative, flexible and responsive to the needs of the learners. That's the purpose of practice.

Preparing to Practice

As you prepare for a practice teaching session, complete these sentence stems and share them with your knowledgeable observer:

- My session topic is…

- The learning objectives are…

- The teaching method(s) I intend to use are…

- With this session, I am confident about my ability to…

- I am working on…

- I feel particularly vulnerable about…

- I'd like specific feedback on…

When choosing an observer, find someone you trust to have your best interest at heart, someone who will be gentle but frank, appreciative yet challenging. Seek out someone who knows the difference between feedback and criticism. (See Jenny Rogers, Fig. 4, page 26) Ask that person to be honest about what went well, and clear about what still needs work. Encourage them to offer no more than two or three key points of feedback, since you probably can't incorporate more than that, especially in the early days with a new teaching method. Let your observer know in advance whether you'd like to receive feedback verbally or in writing. Listen carefully to what your observer has to say. Breathe deeply and stay put if you find yourself tempted to interrupt or debate any of the feedback. And remember, feedback is just feedback. It's not truth, it's one person's perspective. Any feedback you receive is yours to accept or discard, yours to play with and incorporate or reject. Whatever you decide to do with the feedback, it never hurts to hear it.

Giving Feedback

If you are reading this book (and especially if you are preparing to participate in one of KLC's *Teaching Leadership* workshops or conferences), you will no doubt find yourself called upon to offer feedback to a colleague.

When you are in the "knowledgeable observer" role:

1. **INVITE THE PERSON TO SPEAK FIRST.** Jenny Rogers suggests asking for a detailed, nonjudgmental report on what they just did.

2. **BEGIN YOUR FEEDBACK WITH OBSERVATIONS.** "Here's what I saw you do. Here's what I heard you say."

3. **THEN, COMMUNICATE IMPACT.** "When you did this, I felt like that. When you did that I realized this."

4. **ACKNOWLEDGE WHAT WORKED.** Your colleague is taking a risk by practicing in front of you. Support that risk as you would wish to be supported yourself. (According to brain scientist David Rock, people get on average only a couple of minutes of positive feedback each year, versus thousands of hours of negative feedback.)

5. **SUGGEST ONLY ONE OR TWO AREAS FOR IMPROVEMENT.** That's about all most of us can handle in one sitting.

6. **GIVE FEEDBACK. AVOID CRITICISM.**

Feedback vs. Criticism

FEEDBACK	CRITICISM
• Designed to improve performance	• A way of unloading anger or disappointment
• Focused on needs of receiver	• Focused on needs of the giver
• Calm	• Angry, dismissive, emotional
• Accentuates positive first	• Ignore positive
• Tough on the performance	• Tough on the person
• Specific, descriptive, facts	• Vague, generalized, evaluative
• Giver owns opinion	• Attributes opinions to others
• Focuses on the future; suggests positive alternatives	• Looks backward; laments missed opportunities
• Two-way –ask questions about the learner's purpose, experience and opinions	• One-way, pronouncements

Teaching = Leadership

Teaching leadership is itself a challenge that requires all of the attitudes and behaviors introduced in a KLC program. As a teacher and a coach, using the methods described in this book, you will take some personal and professional risks. If you are used to feeling comfortable and in charge when you teach, you might experience a sense of incompetence or discomfort, or even fear, at the start of a class or when you face a new group. You'll need to acknowledge those feelings and perhaps call on colleagues for support. It helps to remind yourself that leadership (conceived of as an action) is seldom comfortable, and that learning depends on the teacher's ability to create an environment in which anyone can lead, from anywhere in the room.

If you are an experienced trainer or coach, the methods contained in this book might require you to stretch the edge of your competence and recommit to the purpose of your work. If you are relatively new to coaching or facilitation, go easy on yourself at first. Start by facilitating the activities and conversations in Chapter 4, and find an experienced partner or trusted mentor to support you as you experiment with the less traditional teaching methods in Chapter 1, 2 and 3.

Whatever your level, as you begin to practice these ideas, continually remind yourself that your purpose is to help others learn and make progress toward larger goals, and that, if you wish to succeed, you might need to let go of habits and approaches that have contributed to your success thus far. If you attend a *Teaching Leadership* offering at KLC, we will help you fine-tune your teaching goals, encourage you to try new things and challenge you to take more risks in the classroom or coaching relationship.

If you commit to practicing the methods outlined in this book, you probably will discover (as we did) that some learners who are accustomed to training that offers stimulating conversation about leadership theory but little encouragement to stretch and try new behaviors will become frustrated as you push them to stop chatting and start doing something to move the group forward. In our workshops, we will support you as you learn to put up with learner discomfort and applaud you as you work hard to become competent in these teaching methods.

Chances are, you were drawn to teaching because you love to learn. We can almost guarantee that you will love engaging with the KLC leadership framework and teaching methods. If you challenge yourself to understand and apply the leadership competencies listed in Figures 1 and 2, and if you learn and practice the teaching methods in Chapters 1 through 4, you will find yourself growing and changing as much or more than your students. You will find that you must stretch yourself, even as you challenge others to apply a new mindset and test new ideas about leadership. As you put these methods into practice, you'll be rewarded by learners who surprise you in the classroom and who discover fresh possibilities for making progress in the midst of a coaching engagement.

These teaching methods require practitioners to let go of being in charge and to hold themselves back from feeding information to students in favor of making space for learners to test ideas, take action and grow in their ability to lead.

What makes these methods
so exciting is they
require practitioners to
APPROACH TEACHING
AS AN ACT OF LEADERSHIP.

The methods contained in this book are not foolproof. In any moment, whatever you try could fizzle or fall flat. A student could misunderstand you. Another could get defensive. Someone else could become confused. But instead of sliding back to your old comfortable way of teaching leadership, you could acknowledge the impasse, figure out what happened, remember your purpose and start again.

If you're not
FAILING REGULARLY,
you're not
ACTING EXPERIMENTALLY.

You're not risking enough. You're not practicing what you preach. Success means that learners understand — because they see you modeling it — that making progress depends on willingness to intervene more often, to experiment, to try new ways of approaching entrenched problems, and to increase the risk of failure. The way we think about it is: "If I fail, I learn. If I learn, that's progress." With that mindset, even setbacks are satisfying, both in the classroom and in the field.

WE TAKE THE LONG VIEW OF DEVELOPING LEADERSHIP.
We know that the world needs countless people capable of mobilizing others to make progress on daunting challenges.

For learners to change behaviors, we teachers of leadership must push ourselves further and further outside our comfort zones. We must lead people to take off their rose-colored glasses and look directly at the gap between the current reality and their aspirations for themselves, their organizations, their businesses, their communities, their governments, and the world. To do so, we have to master teaching methods that are awkward and unusual. At every step of the learning journey, we have to encourage action and accountability.

A New Whole

Each section of this book contains resources to help you deliver meaningful learning experiences. Each was previously published as a small guidebook. Now, we have brought these resources together in a single volume to help you address the gap between your goals and the results you are achieving through your leadership programs. This is more than a summary of what we have produced in the past: It is a progression of methods designed to meet a mission, a set of approaches to create not only learning, but also change.

If you teach leadership, whether full time, just a few hours a month or as a volunteer, you are in the transformational learning business. The methods contained here help you create deep learning experiences. They support your efforts to help others make progress on important challenges.

"Transformative learning," writes Jack Mezirow, the professor of adult and continuing education who coined the term and launched the contemporary discussion of this subject, "refers to the process by which we transform our taken-for-granted frames of reference (meaning perspectives, habits of mind, mindsets) to make them more inclusive, discriminating, open, emotionally capable of change, and reflective so that they may generate beliefs and opinions that will prove more true or justified to guide action."

Building on Mezirow's definition, scholars in "Creating Leaders: An Ontological/Phenomenological Model," have described transformational learning about leadership as providing students with "an opportunity to examine and eliminate the grip of their everyday commonsense worldview and their existing frames of reference relative to leader and leadership."

Our Debt of Gratitude

None of these teaching methods were invented from scratch by the authors of this book or by the teachers of KLC's *Teaching Leadership* offerings. Case-in-Point was pioneered by Harvard University's Kennedy School of Government and introduced to Kansans by Marty Linsky and Kristen Von Donop, who trained and mentored our first faculty members. Our coaching approach is grounded in definitions and competencies developed and tested by the International Coach Federation. Case teaching has a long history in higher education; anyone who wants a deeper dive should research the work of Harvard Business School's C.

Roland Christensen. It was, again, Marty Linsky's case teaching prowess that encouraged KLC to explore and invest in the method.

We hope this book builds on the work of these talented and generous individuals and the organizations they represent, linking their innovations to a set of practical and uniquely challenging leadership principles and competencies and empowering you to re-imagine your approach to helping people learn about leadership.

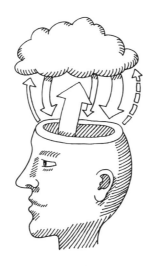

Teacher:
FACILITATOR OF LEARNING, PRACTICE AND GROWTH.

Our Use of the Word Teacher

We have adopted the word "teacher" as an umbrella word that, in this book and for our *Teaching Leadership* series of workshops and conferences, means "facilitator of learning, practice and growth." We recognize at least some of the reasons why this could be a controversial choice, and we hope that it will not be a barrier to your use and enjoyment of this book. Likewise, we have chosen the word "learners" to refer to individuals who, in your context, might be called students, participants, employees, colleagues, group members, etc.

Using the Resources in This Book

KLC promotes an open-source approach to leadership development. We encourage, support and train people who don't work for KLC to use and adapt our curriculum, activities and resources. We want the best and brightest of teachers, trainers, coaches, consultants and facilitators worldwide to use the principles, competencies and teaching methods we have honed to develop leadership capacity in others.

Our open-source approach means you have permission to use KLC ideas in your work. Use our models. Change them. Adapt them. Make them your own. Share our principles and competencies. Follow the session guides in Chapter 4. Ask the coaching questions in Chapter 2. Copy the Case-in-Point tips from Chapter 1 and carry them with you when you teach. In return, we ask three things. First, please give us credit for the ideas. Second, if appropriate, use our "For the Common Good: Participant Handbook" in your courses (available at *www.kansasleadershipcenter.org*). Third, share our website, *www.kansasleadershipcenter.org,* so that people can connect with us if they wish.

CHAPTER 1

Case-in-Point Teaching

Case-in-Point Teaching

Inside a brightly lit meeting room, a teacher stands before a group of about two dozen people scattered around four round tables. Flanked by a pair of flip charts, she feels the tension rising during the first full day of a leadership development program. The group has begun an hour-long discussion of how they might serve as a case study for the leadership principles and competencies posted on the wall at the front of the room.

Watching from a balcony, you would quickly see that something unusual is going on here. This is not a traditional classroom. The teacher is far from the only one talking. She begins with a question designed to gather information about the group and the individuals within it. She frequently makes observations about what is happening in the room. She asks probing questions, allowing long silences as learners consider what to say. When they speak, she listens but does not summarize or actively affirm each learner comment. Instead, she might offer several possible interpretations of a comment or invite group members to share their own guesses about the meaning behind someone's words or actions. Throughout the session, the teacher remains composed, thoughtful, curious and, sometimes, challenging.

A few learners seem confused or frustrated, while a handful drive the conversation. Group members interact with one another, playing off the teacher's observations, questions and interpretations. They have learned to define an intervention as a time when someone acts to influence the group. Some learners look for opportunities to intervene, but others slump in their chairs as if attempting to avoid attention. The mood grows tense. Two individuals disagree. Factions emerge. Not all feel their needs are being met.

In a heated moment among members of the group, the teacher does not shy away from the conflict, nor does she allow it to burn out of control. Instead, she tries to manage it to a productive end, jumping in to reframe the debate and question assumptions. She presses the "pause button" at an especially interesting time and asks the group, "What's going on here?" She invites learners to do the same. "What does it say about this group that only three people are doing most of the talking?" she asks. Later, she says, "I notice that Robert has jumped in several times to defend other members of the group. What role is he playing for the group? How is that role helping or hindering our progress?"

At one point, learners aim their fire at the teacher, criticizing her approach. Those concerns become a Case-in-Point of their own, as she opens her decisions to scrutiny. She interrupts the action to introduce a relevant leadership competency and later seizes a moment to relate a story of her own. However, whether presenting or storytelling, questioning or interpreting, her focus remains squarely on the group and how its interactions illustrate the challenges and opportunities involved in exercising leadership.

Running parallel to the conversation in the room is the conversation the teacher is having within herself. In the midst of the action, she mentally ascends to the balcony, analyzing data about what is going on with the group and weighing her own options for what to do next. Despite her wealth of knowledge about leadership, the teacher's attention remains on what is happening in the moment, in the room. Sometimes things don't go as she expects. One of her questions falls flat. An interpretation about a certain faction proves flawed. In the face of failure, she remains flexible yet persistent. She ascends to the balcony again, reviews the situation more objectively and intervenes again based on the new information she has acquired.

From time to time, one of her fellow teachers intervenes from the back of the room, perhaps highlighting a pattern or dynamic she missed.

All the while, the teacher is managing herself. She breathes deeply to steady herself in the face of conflict. She stays mindful of situations and personality types that might annoy her. She works to manage those triggers by focusing on the purpose of the session and what she wants the group to learn and practice. She leans into uncomfortable moments and doesn't hesitate to share an interpretation that she has never made in a classroom before. She does her best to keep the group in a zone where everyone can learn from the others. As the session comes to a close, she simply acknowledges the time boundary and ends the discussion, releasing the group for a short break and turning over the floor to her colleague for the next session.

What is Case-in-Point?

You've just read about what Case-in-Point teaching looks like from the balcony, the metaphorical place from which we broaden our view of systems and situations. In the rest of the chapter we set out this demanding teaching method, a primary approach to teaching the KLC leadership principles and competencies, that rests on a simple yet provocative idea:

LEADERSHIP, ALTHOUGH DIFFICULT TO TEACH, CAN BE LEARNED IN A DYNAMIC CLASSROOM SETTING

where learners experience the very conditions
that make exercising leadership challenging
in the public and organizational spheres.

Premise and Purpose

We help you understand the levels of attention, common patterns and leadership competencies necessary to have an impact and provide, in Figures 7–16, useful tools to help you plan and execute Case-in-Point sessions. In Chapter 4 we provide outlines for eight content sessions; however, for the most part we assume that by the time you set yourself the challenge of using the Case-in-Point method, you are already well-versed in the KLC competencies or some other approach to leadership on adaptive challenges.

The idea behind Case-in-Point is that learning about leadership requires more than taking in information or digesting concepts. In today's increasingly complex, unpredictable and interdependent world, traditional methods alone will not work. If we are to teach adults to exercise leadership more effectively, we must give them a chance to experience the challenges of leadership in real time.

Case-in-Point requires teachers to view a group as more than a collection of individuals. Instead, the class explores itself as a social system, one whose dynamics tend to mimic patterns in the larger social environment. Case-in-Point is based on the premise that learners bring with them to the classroom all of the promises and persistent problems faced by the company or community they represent.

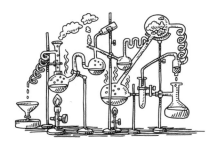

LEARNERS NEED A CLASSROOM LABORATORY
WHERE THEY CAN TAKE RISKS, EXPERIMENT AND
REFLECT ON THE IMPACT OF NEW BEHAVIORS.

KLC's listening tour of the state in 2007 revealed a culture marked by a few "usual" voices dominating the discourse while the majority stayed silent. We heard about a pervasive us-versus-them mentality dividing those with authority and those without, a status quo that gets in the way of addressing extremely complex, difficult problems. To make progress on big challenges, such as thriving in a global marketplace or eliminating poverty in a community, 21st-century institutions need individuals who are willing to engage across factions and deal with the conflict that comes with making difficult, value-laden decisions. This kind of leadership depends less on formal authority and more on skill and personal credibility. Individuals must demonstrate the flexibility and inner fortitude to strategically weather the storms of conflict, human emotion and loss in purposefully pursuing lasting solutions to big challenges.

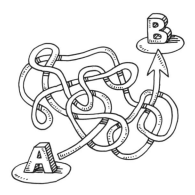

You have the opportunity — in a unique environment created in collaboration with your learners — to orchestrate confrontations that place a group's

ASSUMPTIONS AND INTERACTIONS

in stark contrast with its

ASPIRATIONS AND IDEALS.

Groups not only confront the ways in which their own behaviors reflect or contribute to a less than ideal reality, but also try on new, potentially more effective behaviors. Using the leadership principles and competencies as a guide, learners practice intervening in new ways, building capacity to make progress on things they care about. As you might have guessed, guiding a group through such a difficult learning process is no easy task (see Figure 5). The basic steps for a session are simple (see Figure 6) but require practice and artistry. In a Case-in-Point session, learners are asked to leave behind some of what they know and hold dear. Many adults who attend leadership programs have been rewarded for the way they currently behave, and others are happy wielding authority in situations where acts of leadership are required.

You have the opportunity — in a unique environment created in collaboration with your learners — to orchestrate confrontations that place a group's assumptions and interactions in stark contrast with its aspirations and ideals.

Your role in the classroom puts you in the position of challenging people, prodding them to try new behaviors and consider a different way of relating to the world. Your job is to encourage successful adults to risk failure and embarrassment, or even shame, for the sake of learning and growth. In such a situation, some will become confused, uncomfortable or even angry. It almost goes without saying that using this teaching method represents an adaptive challenge that resists easy solutions. You will need to learn new things and make unaccustomed demands on yourself as a teacher. You will need to exercise leadership skillfully from the front of the room and depend on the same from colleagues who support you from the back of the room.

Case-in-Point compels you as an instructor to

MODEL THE LEADERSHIP COMPETENCIES THAT YOU ARE TRYING TO TEACH.

To use Case-in-Point effectively, you must be purposeful, provocative and intentional in your interventions. You will be guiding learners through a process with no easy answers, a journey with no road map. You will need to give up a significant portion of your control and authority to enable group members to work the issues in the room effectively. This act of sharing authority with the learners is perhaps the fundamental

Common Challenges of Case-in-Point

- Keep the focus on the "here and now."

- Stay in a diagnostic mentality and model it for learners.

- Continually violate learners' expectation that they can rely on authority for the answers.

- Frustrate learners' thirst for technical solutions, tools and tactics.

- Fight against teaching defaults, such as disseminating content or information.

- Reveal and test hidden issues, assumptions and interpretations.

- Direct attention to tough, systemic interpretations.

- Read situations, and design and execute interventions in the moment.

- Hold steady when learners express discomfort or hostility.

- Resist the urge to provide closure.

- Focus on systemic conflicts rather than scapegoating individuals or offering benign interpretations.

- Make conscious choices about which cases to pursue and which to let pass.

- Know when to persist and when to let go of a case.

- Choose when, whether and how to accept "casualties" among learners.

- Engage, provoke, support and challenge learners all at the same time.

FIGURE 6:

Framework for a Case-in-Point Session

1. Know which leadership principle or competency you want to teach (see Figures 1 and 2).

2. Engage your group and get them interacting with some minimal sense of shared purpose.

- That shared purpose may be as broad as "learning about leadership," "applying new leadership skills to make progress on eliminating poverty" or "practicing new leadership skills to help our company succeed," or as narrow as "learning and practicing diagnosing the situation we are in" or "learning how to get a group to work productively together."

- Typically you'll need to get the group going with a question, observation or activity.

3. Shine the light on a moment, pattern or dynamic that could relate to the leadership idea you are trying to teach.

- This moment becomes the case.

- You may interject a comment or question or pause the action for a longer discussion.

4. Use the case you have illuminated to encourage or provoke group members to practice leadership skills.

- For instance, if you are teaching the competency Manage Self, you could first highlight a moment when someone experimented outside his or her comfort zone, then explore the impact on the group and invite others to do the same.

5. Debrief and invite learners to reflect on how to apply the ideas in the real world.

- How and when you debrief depends on the level of disequilibrium you wish to generate among learners (see Figure 14).

- The more often you debrief, the less disequilibrium will remain. Some groups can handle more, some less.

intervention in Case-in-Point teaching, and it can be profoundly disturbing to group members who are oriented to expect protection, direction and order from the authority figure standing before them.

This style of teaching also represents a significant stretch for many teachers, particularly those who are used to more traditional presentation or facilitation. Your primary role in Case-in-Point is not to provide answers or closure; rather, your job is to stimulate deeper thinking and create the environment in which learners can work productively together to practice new approaches to leadership. At its simplest, Case-in-Point is the process of directing a group's attention to teachable moments, then holding collective focus on those moments long enough for individuals to engage themselves and one another in new and productive ways.

*Making observations and interpretations
in the midst of the action is your core task.*

THE TEACHER IS CONTINUALLY MOVING FROM THE "DANCE FLOOR" TO "THE BALCONY,"

*seeking an objective view of what is happening
with the group. From that metaphorical vantage
point, you interpret data, recognize patterns,
and use your experience and intuition to choose
a leadership "case" for the class to study.*

Diagnosis Mindset

The first step toward creating the necessary environment in your classroom is cultivating your own diagnostic skills. Case-in-Point requires that you observe, question and interpret what is going on in the room, even as you intervene.

In "Leadership Can Be Taught," Sharon Daloz Parks writes that with Case-in-Point everything that happens is potential "grist for the learning mill." Each interaction is a source of material for learning about leadership. So, Case-in-Point teaching involves mastering three diagnostic skills:

1. Observing potential learning opportunities;

2. Recognizing their implications related to the teaching topic; and

3. Making quick, conscious choices about where to direct the attention of the group.

Levels of Attention

Michael Johnstone and Maxime Fern of Vantage Point Consulting recommend cultivating four "levels of attention." The first level, individual behavior, focuses on patterns related to a single learner. At this level, the teacher might notice whether one person's comments are holding the attention of the group. A second level involves interpersonal relationships, or patterns that occur during exchanges involving two or more learners. This may take the form of certain individuals constantly agreeing or disagreeing with one another. A third level of attention focuses on patterns that emerge in the group and system as a whole — for instance, how the group responds to the absence of authority. The fourth level, context, explores issues related to the composition of the group, the setting, societal pressures or other circumstances under which the group has been operating. A teacher who pays attention at this fourth level might, for instance, pause and notice that a group of CEOs seems skeptical of the principle that "leadership is an activity, not a position." Whatever level you are attending to, your diagnostic tasks are to observe what is happening, imagine reasons why it might be happening (or ask learners to speak up with their own interpretations) and take an educated guess about whether what you have noticed might make a good case for learning about leadership.

Diagnosing at Four Levels of Attention

LEVEL 1

Individual

What is that person doing, and why?

LEVEL 2

Interpersonal

What is the pattern of behavior between individuals, and why is it occurring?

LEVEL 3

System

What dynamics and patterns are at play in this room?

LEVEL 4

Context

What outside forces are affecting this group?

Learning about leadership is adaptive work, which requires moving beyond simple explanations. Despite the pressure that comes with diagnosing situations in the moment, it is important for teachers to test multiple interpretations of the patterns they see emerging. This approach creates multiple choice points for engaging learners and might enable you to pursue alternate tacks in rapid succession to arrive at a learning moment. As you observe patterns, take time to explore tough interpretations. Push for interpretations that are difficult or uncomfortable for group members to talk about and that provoke conflict. Encourage learners to make interpretations about dynamics in the group and what the system as a whole needs to accomplish to make progress.

A perfect case for beginning teachers using this method is the case of the group that doesn't want to admit what is really going on.

FIND A CASE WHERE YOU CAN HELP PEOPLE PRACTICE "NAMING THE ELEPHANT,"

invite them to engage with that elephant more honestly and directly and give them feedback about what's effective in the moment. Thus, you use Case-in-Point teaching to give learners experience and skills that will help them wherever they might live, work or volunteer.

Johnstone and Fern note that moving beyond the individual and relationship levels of attention can be difficult for teachers. "It is, therefore, useful," they write, "to consider that individual and interpersonal issues emerge in groups because they represent something in the group about one of four things: their common purpose (or lack thereof); the pace and focus of the work; the assumptions and values held individually or collectively; and the needs and fears that people hold." For instance, rather than voice and deal with lack of shared purpose or competing values, group members might resort to forming unspoken alliances, scapegoating, competing for the attention of authority or other unproductive behaviors, all of which are clues that one or more of these common issues is alive in your group. It may be an act of leadership for you to name these behaviors and suggest interpretations that go beyond individuals behaving badly, encouraging the group to consider systemic and contextual interpretations.

Common Classroom Patterns and Personalities

{ **RELIANCE ON AUTHORITY** }

The group (or members of the group) depends
on authority to provide the answers or reacts negatively
to a lack of protection, direction and order.

{ **TAKING THE CONVERSATION OUT OF THE ROOM** }

The group or certain members resist
using themselves as the source of data.

{ **THE SILENT HALF, THE VOCAL FEW** }

Most learners remain silent while a handful
of learners dominate the conversation.

{ **THE SUBSTITUTE AUTHORITY** }

A learner steps in to restore protection, direction and order
by calling on others in the cohort or appointing a facilitator.

{ **THE RESCUER** }

A learner takes on the role of explaining away
the disequilibrium of others or defending their actions.

{ **LACK OF TRUST AND SECURITY** }

Group members claim they do not know one another
well enough to explore how they function as a system.

{ **THE TIME BOUNDARY** }

The response of learners to nearing the end of a session,
such as inserting comments near boundaries because
they are less likely to be challenged.

{ **TAKING IT TO THE PARKING LOT** }

Concerns or conflicts not voiced during the session are
discussed afterward, often by people who share a point of view.
We call this "Kansas nice."

Identifying patterns within a group can be difficult if you don't know what to look for. Figure 10, "Data-Gathering Questions," may be useful as you begin practicing Case-in-Point teaching to guide your observations and interpretations of how the group is functioning as a system.

Using Leadership Skills while Practicing Case-in-Point

Always remember that Case-in-Point is based on the idea that the group reflects the larger society: All of the things that make leadership difficult with people back home are in the room. Your job is to bring them to the surface and use them to facilitate learning. All the data you need are already in the room, waiting to be unearthed and interpreted.

You will likely make mistakes or misinterpret data. This method forces you to consciously choose between being perfect and being effective. Keep pushing yourself to the edge of your comfort zone, where you are bound to make mistakes in service of generating learning for the group. If you accept the premise that learning about leadership is an adaptive challenge, then maintaining an experimental mindset and continually learning from unsuccessful interventions are important aspects of this work.

Managing Self while Facilitating Learning

Although a heightened level of systemic awareness is a key success factor when facilitating Case-in-Point, it is certainly not the only ingredient. Even as you become proficient at recognizing patterns and using them as learning moments for your group, you must also hone your ability to monitor your own impulses and understand how your actions and demeanor affect the group. Likewise, you must learn to stomach the considerable uncertainty that comes with this method. To be successful, you will need to provoke and push the group forward in ways most people have never encountered in a classroom. Your goal is to create situations in the room that replicate patterns of interactions that participants recognize. You want learners to notice similarities between what is happening in the classroom and unproductive behavior they see in meetings at work or in community organizations. At the same time, you'll need to energize group members, encouraging them to work together to make progress on learning about leadership. The dimensions listed in Figure 2 under the competency Manage Self are useful reminders of what it takes to be successful with this method.

Remember, too, these diagnostic and self-management skills demand practice. Don't wait until you are in the classroom to think about the four levels of attention or consider the many ways in which learners might pull your triggers. Be prepared. Practice awareness wherever you go. Intervene in more provocative ways in your family, volunteer work and team meetings. Most of all, take every opportunity to observe and partner with experienced practitioners of this method.

As you observe master-users of this method, you will notice the personal presence they bring to the task of building a bridge between themselves and the people they teach. This quality is easy to identify but difficult to fully explain. With Case-in-Point, presence involves being poised and purposeful enough to hold a group, including yourself as the teacher, through the adaptive work of learning about leadership. Parks describes presence as imagining "one's self as a resonant and responsive node in a dynamic network or field of energy and an agent of emergent possibility and progress." In Case-in-Point, you as the teacher do not develop the content and cannot know exactly what new learning will arise, but your strong presence inspires trust in the process. The type of presence Parks describes also helps you to avoid being swamped by emotions, both the learners' and your own.

Managing yourself and maintaining presence requires an understanding of where your strengths lie, what your vulnerabilities are, and what situations and personalities tend to take you out of the game. When we suggest that you make tough interpretations, that means naming behaviors and group dynamics that we often do not mention in polite conversation. For example, when you offer a possible interpretation that some group members are unconsciously working together to silence a minority voice, you need to feel confident that you can deal with any emotions that arise and, in the midst of those emotions, that you can push the group to practice leadership behaviors, such as continuing to examine that interpretation or identifying another that is even more provocative. Case-in-Point carries considerable risks for any teacher, because many choices that must be made during your teaching sessions are value-laden. For many, provoking discomfort and hostility or appearing incompetent in front of a large group while in an authority role feels embarrassing, to say the least.

Because of the "in the moment" nature of Case-in-Point, which defies the use of a structured game plan,

YOU WILL RARELY KNOW YOUR NEXT MOVE BEFORE IT IS UPON YOU.

For even the most experienced teachers, that is scary.

Practicing Case-in-Point means learning to deal with these uncertainties and diligently maintaining the separation between your sense of self and your understanding of your role. When learners express frustration or anger toward you as teacher during Case-in-Point, it's not personal. They are responding to the role you play. Your teaching role involves creating and managing distress. When you defy expectations of authority and, instead of providing information, attempt to lead people through an adaptive, experiential learning process, you become the focal point of anxieties about whether they will be able to keep up with peers or perform adequately in the classroom. In these situations, it helps to take a deep breath, glance at your colleague at the back of the room for support and remind yourself not to take these attacks personally. They are a symptom of systemic distress and might be exactly what the group needs to make progress on the difficult work of learning about leadership.

Your interventions in Case-in-Point are a series of experiments based on interpretations of available data. When an intervention does not go as planned, you can waste time blaming yourself for the mistake, or you can celebrate that you now have additional data to inform your next interventions. When done well, Case-in-Point creates a forum in which learners can practice leadership in real time. Putting the KLC leadership principles and competencies into action requires a sense of curiosity and an experimental mindset.

Above all, remember that teachers model leadership by making conscious choices about whether, when and how to intervene skillfully. Observations, questions, interpretations and provocative action are what Heifetz and Linsky refer to as the "straightforward tactics of leadership."

Observations

An observation is a simple statement that directs attention to actions, patterns, dynamics or existing conditions in the room ("I observed that many people were looking around the room, checking their cell phones or talking to someone else while James was speaking"). This category of intervention is typically less risky than others because it is merely a snapshot of the group's interactions. With it you essentially call a timeout and shift learners to the balcony, where they can explore the meaning of what you offered.

Questions

The teacher can use questions to invite learners to make observation of their own ("What have you observed about how group members are responding to James's comments?"). After a few people have made observations, you can shift to questions about interpretations ("What does it say about this group that James was not able to hold everyone's attention?" Or, more provocatively, "What about James's point of view is this group afraid to tackle?").

Questions engage the group in gathering data and exploring the deeper meanings of a moment or interaction. Your constant, curious questions are crucial to the success of a Case-in-Point session. Used skillfully, curious questions direct attention to hidden dynamics that may be impeding progress. As these dynamics are revealed, group members learn and practice skills for moving beyond them.

Data-gathering questions (Figure 10) are the foundation of effective Case-in-Point. Oftentimes, the teacher enters knowing little about what's really going on in the room. Data-gathering questions, particularly those that expose conflictual dynamics, help generate content for the session.

The best data-gathering questions invite learners to reveal their purpose, goals, fears, state of mind, membership in a faction, etc. In poker parlance, these questions force group members to "show their hands." Try pairing data-gathering questions with an activity, such as reflective writing or asking participants to write their responses to your questions on a whiteboard. (For instance, you might pose the question, "To what extent is today's learning meeting your needs?" and then say, "Please come up to the board and respond to that question on this scale of 1 to 10, with 1 being 'not at all' and 10 being 'to a great extent.'")

Interpretations

Your interpretations, possible explanations of why certain patterns are occurring, should push learners' thinking to the right side of the Technical/Adaptive Mindshift chart (see Figure 21, page 206). Your task in Case-in-Point is to model the way toward a more adaptive approach to leadership by making inherently provocative or conflictual interpretations that move learners into a productive zone of work. ("One interpretation might be that older, experienced participants in the group doubt the credibility of younger members, like James.") We use the phrase "raising the heat" in this context to mean getting a group fired up enough to start learning in a new way. Conflictual interpretations make hidden issues more transparent and available for exploration by the group, but they can also prompt strong adverse reactions because people typically hate having their actions interpreted unless the interpretation shows them in a positive light.

FIGURE 9:

Types of Interventions

Observations

"Here's exactly what
I saw happen."

Questions

"What is going on here?"

Interpretations

"One interpretation of
what just happened is…"

Provocative action

Pauses, Requests, Interrupting,
Ignoring, Silence

FIGURE 10:

Data-Gathering Questions

1. **WHO HAS THE GROUP'S ATTENTION? WHO DOESN'T?**
Who speaks (or does not speak) when, about what, to whom,
how often? How much influence do actions have?

2. **HOW WELL IS THE GROUP FUNCTIONING?**
How are individuals harnessing the whole group versus
advocating independent positions?

3. **ARE THEY INTEGRATING NEW VIEWS,
SEPARATING INTO FACTIONS OR ADOPTING
A SINGLE VIEWPOINT?**
What patterns are visible in the group's interactions?

4. **HOW WELL ARE LEARNER NEEDS BEING MET?**
How much is the group interacting? Are people being inclusive
or controlling or acknowledging or recognizing others?

5. **WHAT ROLES ARE BEING PLAYED IN THE GROUP?**
What responses do learners have when the heat rises?

FIGURE 11:

Ways to Gather Data

ASK A QUESTION (OR CONDUCT AN EXERCISE)
THAT BROADLY PROMPTS LEARNERS:

To reveal the faction they identify with most or least.
*Example: Who here expects to be employed with this organization
in 10 years?*

**To disclose their present state of mind and the anxieties they
have in the moment.**
*Example: To what extent are you willing to be vulnerable right now?
Mark on a scale of 1 to 10, with 10 being completely willing and 1 being
completely unwilling.*

To tell the story about themselves in this moment.

**To reveal their expectations about the work that is asked of them
in the room.**

To disclose a perceived strength, vulnerability or trigger.

**To expose a default behavior (such as their typical approach
to conflict).**

To reveal deeply held values, fundamental aspects of their identities.

To disclose a potential loss they could experience.

To explain the level of care they expect.

One particularly effective intervention is naming the factions in the
room. When you use your position of authority to put people in groups
according to your interpretations of what they value, learners sit up
and listen. They jump in to debate the accuracy of their teacher's
interpretations. (For support with naming factions, see the Faction Map
in the "For the Common Good: Participant Handbook," and the session
description in this book.)

Unless it is your intention to conduct a particularly provocative Case-in-
Point session (what we refer to as a "high-heat" session), it is useful
to express interpretations as hypotheses, as only one of many possible

ways of making meaning of the moment ("One interpretation is…" or "I am curious about whether this means… "). Posing your idea this way opens the door for learners to join the conversation and practice the diagnostic skill of making tough interpretations. Encourage learners to take the same open-door approach with their own interpretations. Teaching them to rent rather than own interpretations and to invite fellow learners to offer another point of view helps people deal with not-quite-noble explanations for behavior and patterns and remain involved long enough to thoroughly vet hidden issues.

A POINT OF CAUTION:

Initially, most learners will confuse observations and interpretations. Take time to make the distinction clear. Help learners practice making observations about what they can see, hear, taste or touch before allowing them to move on to ascribing meaning (interpretations) to what they've observed.

Provocative Actions

Provocative actions are a category of direct interventions that teachers can make in Case-in-Point. These include hitting the pause button to stop the action. Once you've paused the action, you can metaphorically rewind the tape and invite learners to review the last few minutes of conversation. As they discuss what just happened, your role is to look for an interesting case, name it, and ask the group to explore leadership lessons within.

Another set of provocative actions are requests that enrich discussion by jostling learners out of their comfort zones. For instance, you might request that group members divide themselves based on whether they consider themselves liberal or conservative, or split into three groups based on how much they are learning about leadership from today's sessions. Requests such as these can raise the heat and accelerate experiential learning, but you also run the risk of being accused of artificially provoking conflict.

You may also intervene directly by interrupting speakers, cutting off conversation at a time boundary or ignoring an individual's questions or comments. Use provocative actions consciously and purposefully. The more Case-in-Point centers on your actions, the fewer opportunities there are for learners to practice leadership skills themselves.

Silence is another useful form of provocative action. The act of being fully present with the group, yet saying nothing, may allow the gravity of a question or interpretation to sink in. It may serve the purpose of engaging less talkative learners by offering them space in the conversation. It can also raise the heat by disturbing people's expectations of authority and increasing the pressure on them to fill the void themselves. On your best days, learners will fill the void by experimenting with new leadership behaviors. On other days, the silence will be broken only by laughter and furtive glances.

In practice, you will use all the above interventions in different combinations throughout a session. Determining which interventions represent the proper course is an experimental process driven by your diagnosis of what the group needs in the moment. Your goal is to get them to practice mobilizing others to make progress on learning about leadership. At times you will be stuck and won't know what to do. Figure 12 provides a list of options to get you back on track.

Through it all, be mindful of regulating the level of individual and collective distress. The temperature in the room needs to be high enough to spur productive work, but you don't want so much anxiety that people can't think straight or be compassionate with one another. Remember you are building a container strong enough to hold learners while they do the work of practicing leadership behaviors that are new to them.

Potential Moves in Case-in-Point

Call attention to discrepancies between content (what is being said) and patterns of behavior.

Focus on one participant.

Start or use "timeouts" for written reflection.

Use silence.

Collect data about learners ("Whose heat is low right now?"). Ask for a show of hands.

Name a faction in the room. Ask people to identify the factions into which they fall.

Choose your actions based on what you diagnose the group needs vs. what you planned.

Ask a learner to do difficult work; support the learner through difficult work.

Wrap-up/tie learning into KLC leadership concepts.

Bring attention back to what's happening in the room.

Identify intuition and emotions.

Admit "I'm stuck" to help get the group going.

Make a provocative statement (whether or not you hold it as a valid interpretation).

Ask one learner to give another interpretation (and another and another).

Identify "elephants in the room."

Use labels or other behaviors to raise the heat. Even riskier: Name-calling or interrupting to raise the heat.

Honor time boundaries.

Ask permission to stay on a case when a person is hurting.

Offer a systemic or contextual interpretation to redirect attention away from individual interpretations.

THE ZONE OF PRODUCTIVE WORK
*is the place where there is enough heat
to keep people engaged and learning,
but not so much that they shut down.*

As you manage the distress of the group (not too much, not too little), use yourself as a barometer. You are part of the system. Make interpretations about the temperature based on your own gut feelings. Then choose an observation, interpretation, question or provocative action to test your intuition against responses from other members of the system.

Building Trust, Transferring Energy

Case-in-Point requires no one particular style or approach. Your style may tend toward the provocative side, relishing the thrill of challenging assumptions. Or you may appear more contemplative or nurturing. Or perhaps learners find your approach disquieting, full of profound questions and long silences. The most effective teachers maintain some degree of balance between extremes, doing what the moment calls for rather than adopting a manner that is abrasive or predictable and, thus easier to sideline or ignore.

However you approach the work, your task is to inspire and create space for others to learn and practice. After all, although this chapter focuses on how a teacher can use this method effectively, the success of Case-in-Point ultimately rests with the learners. Do they engage, or don't they? Do they stretch outside their comfort zones, or don't they?

"An absolute prerequisite is a real, honest desire to absolutely be curious."

That means being curious not only about what you see, but also about the internal thoughts, emotions and sensations people in the room experience along the way.

Your expression of curiosity through observations, questions, interpretations and provocative actions is an important way to build and transfer energy among learners. Your curiosity infuses the work with purpose, inspiring others to be just as inquisitive about "what's going on here?" It is also one of the factors that makes teaching Case-in-Point as much art as skill.

In the words of Sharon Daloz Parks, artistry implies a "capacity for creative improvisation." When it comes to exercising leadership, artistry implies the willingness to work on the edge of your competence as Picasso did with his painting, and to engage in interdependent relationships with your learners, as musicians and actors do every time they take the stage. Regardless of whether you can sculpt, paint or write, you can aspire to artistry by leading a group (and yourself) to a place where they can practice new leadership behaviors.

This sort of artistry doesn't come without dangers. Like the chiseling of a sculpture, the creation of a new form requires leaving something behind. These losses can be quite painful, for both the group and individual. Once-cherished values or approaches suddenly become expendable. Sometimes there will be casualties who end up being left behind. The art of teaching leadership requires us to name the losses at hand and provide the space for mourning as a bridge to a future where progress becomes more attainable.

The Ground Rules

The pursuit of artistry is not enough to ready you for the adaptive challenge of teaching leadership using this method. Because of the unusual, provocative nature of Case-in-Point teaching, your groups need a set of clearly understood ground rules to help guide them through the stresses of learning.

FIGURE 13:

Case-in-Point Ground Rules

Maintain confidentiality.

Protect voices that raise
difficult issues.

Use cases solely for the purpose
of learning about leadership.

Value authenticity and learning
over politeness.

Stay curious.

Confidentiality is a core ground rule that implies whatever occurs in the room remains with the group. Unless everyone feels assured that teachers and learners alike will honor confidentiality, individuals will find it difficult to muster the courage to be authentically vulnerable in trying new behaviors and getting feedback from you and their peers. This is crucial, because for Case-in-Point to be effective, learners need to begin making their silent assumptions and interpretations, even the distasteful ones, transparent and testable for the group.

When a member raises an uncomfortable issue, groups often attempt to explain away or ignore the insight. Thus, you make learning more likely when you protect voices that raise difficult issues for the group. You can do this by intervening in ways that force the group to confront rather than gloss over a conflictual interpretation. Those who publicly deviate from the group's norms play a beneficial role, fueling creativity by compelling learners to confront ideas or assumptions the system has been working hard to keep hidden.

Another ground rule is that anytime the group is discussing a case, it should be solely for the purposes of learning about leadership. Never use Case-in-Point as sport or to make any individual (including you) look good or bad.

ENCOURAGE LEARNERS TO LISTEN TO ONE ANOTHER AND BE RESPECTFUL, BUT ALSO TO VALUE AUTHENTICITY AND LEARNING OVER POLITENESS.

Also, warn learners that Case-in-Point will be more heated than traditional teaching or facilitated discussion. Encourage them not to take the conflict that emerges personally. Still, no amount of written or verbal explanation will fully prepare some learners for the experience of Case-in-Point; therefore, managing a group's distress is an essential aspect of using the method. We often remind learners who want to make the most of their experience to stay curious in the face of anger, frustration and confusion.

Partnership in Case–in–Point:
The Teacher at the Back of the Room

Case-in-Point is collaborative work. Don't go it alone. To do so would reinforce a lone-wolf model of leadership and would be inconsistent with the leadership principles in Figure 1.

Having a partner at the back of the room — a fellow teacher — doubles the opportunities for observation and interpretation, allows you (at the front of the room) to be more effective and preserves the integrity of the environment. You are a human being and, no matter how hard you work to see and understand, you have blind spots that keep you from seeing what is going on, managing yourself, intervening skillfully and energizing everyone in the room. A back-of-the-room partner closely observes the action, sees your interventions (and how learners respond) from a different perspective, identifies opportunities and purposefully intervenes to highlight learning moments you miss.

Back-row interventions are most effective when they are intended to generate conflict or shift the work from the front-of-room teacher back to the learning group. These might be observations about group dynamics, interpretations that move beyond the benign, or a quick interjection to name a faction taking shape within the group. Offering these interventions in the form of a question is an effective approach, because questions tend not to sideline the main teacher, yet work to generate energy and engagement from the group.

Your partner also serves as a resource after the session, working with you to debrief the session and help you understand why some interventions worked and others did not. Because so much of Case-in-Point teaching involves provoking learners to reflect on their leadership actions, it only makes sense that you would make time to reflect on your actions as a teacher. Your back-of-the-room partner spends more time on the balcony and is a source of valuable feedback on how you played your role in the system.

Regulating the Heat in Case-in-Point

You will need to work with your partner to decide how much discomfort, conflict and uncertainty (about learning outcomes and the role of authority) your group can handle. Use this chart to help you make design decisions and hold to purpose during sessions.

FIGURE 14:

INDICATOR AREA	HIGH HEAT	MEDIUM HEAT	LOW HEAT
Source of content	Nearly all content comes from within the room.	Some content from within the room; some from taught curriculum or outside experiences.	Content from within the room at strategic points.
Where the work happens	Heavy emphasis on what is going on below the neck.	Work frequently shifts from above to below the neck.	Frequently analytical, with some work below the neck.
What is going on emotionally (below the neck)	Group largely responsible for establishing its purpose and directing its work.	Group often directs own purpose with skillful teacher guidance.	Teacher directs group while confounding some expectations of authority.
Role of teacher	Functions as especially purposeful participant; constantly works to share leadership.	Balances role of senior authority with purposeful sharing of leadership.	Intervenes to share leadership but often deploys authority.
Provocativeness	Group names defaults, hidden dynamics, factions, assumptions or heated interactions, including class, race or gender differences.	Teacher purposefully names group and individual dynamics, defaults, factions or hidden assumptions.	Teacher stimulates curiosity about defaults, interesting behaviors/ exchanges or factions and hidden assumptions.
Focus of interpretations	Nearly all time is spent on conflictual interpretations.	Group is asked to elevate but not always own conflictual interpretations.	Group is encouraged to formulate conflictual interpretations as modeled by teacher.
Tolerance of loss/casualties	Group and teacher are willing to manage casualties and move on.	Loss and casualties may be accepted, but permanent and irreversible casualties are avoided.	The intensity only rarely builds up high enough to create the risk of casualties or loss.
Closure and disequilibrium	Individual sessions are typically not brought to a close, and the group may be purposefully left in high disequilibrium.	Sessions are sometimes left open-ended; other times, the teacher provides closure to ensure adequate learning.	Teacher brings sessions to a close to manage the group's feelings of disequilibrium.
Applicability	Learners consciously experiment with competencies in the heat of the moment.	Learners take smart, small risks experimenting with competencies.	Learners start to internalize competencies as a way of being.

alcony

;elf to use the Case-in-Point method by reading a
Sooner or later, you have to jump in and teach, but
ı classroom without practicing first. What to do? You
ng Leadership workshop, and we hope you will. But
ficient practice. What, then?

One additional way to practice Case-in-Point is to use this book as a
guide for examining your daily interactions. Use this chapter to focus
your attention and develop your awareness of system dynamics as they
happen around you. Build a balcony from whence you can observe,
interpret, create questions and visualize a variety of interventions in
your life.

David Chrislip, co-author of "For the Common Good: Redefining Civic
Leadership," has observed that it takes time to develop the heightened
level of systemic awareness necessary for Case-in-Point teaching.
New teachers struggle, along with learners, through a series of
developmental stages until they reach a point where they can effectively
diagnose how a group is functioning as a system. From there, they can
intervene to influence its progress and learning.

At first, you might develop an academic understanding of the method
but have difficulty translating it into practice. Then, pieces start
to come together. You're able to stay on the balcony long enough
to notice patterns of individual behavior or consistent interactions
between two group members. You try intervening to raise the heat but
fail to influence much of anything. As you get comfortable ascending
to the balcony (where observations and interpretations come easiest)
and then descending to the dance floor (where you intervene with
questions and provocative action), you begin to notice the subtleties of
a group's interactions. As you practice Case-in-Point, in the classroom
and as you go about your life, you will become increasingly skilled at
recognizing what is collective work (for instance, agreeing on common
purpose), what are individual needs (to be valued, seen as competent,
to serve as the group caretaker or protector, etc.), the purposes of
each learner (keep my job, change the world, make things happen,
etc.) and the interplay among these drivers of progress. You will find

yourself able to quickly connect what's happening in the room to ideas about leadership. Then you are on your way.

In the end, mastering the Case-in-Point method happens in and out of the classroom, through not only conscious practice, but also your attempts to exercise leadership at work, with your family or in your community. KLC uses Case-in-Point to teach people about leadership. The same cues and skill sets that make Case-in-Point teaching effective are useful when exercising leadership in any system. If you want to succeed, you need to figure out what's going on, decide what the challenges are, and take action to help people learn, grow and make progress on what they care about.

Questions to Ask During Case-in-Point

Purposeful, provocative questions drive the Case-in-Point method and help focus learning outcomes, even as you and your partner remain flexible and curious and share the work of learning with the whole group. The following questions are grouped according to the KLC leadership principles and competencies. Pose these questions aloud for the group to grapple with and use them to make your own silent diagnoses.

FIGURE 15:

Leadership Principles

LEADERSHIP IS AN ACTIVITY, NOT A POSITION.

- How does the group react to my use of authority?
- Who in this group has authority? How does that show up?

ANYONE CAN LEAD, ANYTIME, ANYWHERE.

- Whose work is this?
- Who in the room is using authority?
- Who is exercising leadership?
- What are the responses to acts of leadership?

IT STARTS WITH YOU AND MUST ENGAGE OTHERS.

- Who has attempted to engage someone else?

YOUR PURPOSE MUST BE CLEAR.

- Who has a clear purpose?
- How has a clear sense of purpose affected this group?

IT'S RISKY.

- What's at risk here?
- What would make the risk worthwhile?

Leadership Competencies

DIAGNOSE SITUATION

- To what extent is the group considering conflictual or systemic interpretations?
- What interpretations are we as a group dismissing?
- What concerns you the most about our work together during this week?
- What individual purposes do you see reflected in the behavior of others?
- Is there a shared purpose in the room right now?
- What interpretations can you make about differing responses to distress in the room?

    What dynamics won't this group bring to the surface?

    What conflictual interpretations exist for why we are behaving this way?

    What are some less noble or uglier interpretations of our behavior?
- What work are we trying to avoid?

MANAGE SELF

- At what point have you been triggered?
- How will you find out what story others are telling about you?
- What competing values are at play in the room?
- How do we react when someone speaks from the heart or speaks to loss?
- What will you do to move beyond your comfort zone?

INTERVENE SKILLFULLY

- Whose interventions or acts of leadership in the room are generating responses?
- Whose interventions or acts of leadership in the room are being dismissed or ignored?
- What reactions do you observe when the heat is raised?
- Who is acting experimentally?

ENERGIZE OTHERS

- What factions exist within this room?
- What losses, either real or perceived, are at stake in the room?
- How might we speak to those losses?
- What is this group's collective purpose?

CHAPTER 2

Teaching Case Studies

Teaching Case Studies

It starts with a simple yet provocative question from the teacher, one initially greeted by silence in the room. Some learners start thumbing through the text in front of them, the story of a real-life decision-making dilemma. They dig for clues, starting to form a response. Others stare straight ahead, wondering who will dare to go first.

After breathing in the query for a few seconds, one group member attempts a response. Others join in, one comment leading to the next.

A series of responses evolves into a robust discussion. Learners analyze the material and offer interpretations. They start to disagree and question one another, fleshing out ideas in the process. Factions form, preferring a particular course of action. Tension builds as group members sort out competing ideas and prescriptions.

As it all unfolds, the teacher observes the interaction, interprets the direction of the discussion and intervenes to focus or direct it forward. Acting as a careful listener and observer, the teacher is mindful of not just the discussion's content but also the overall climate and behavior of individual participants.

Although skilled case study teachers leave much of the analytical work to the discussion group, their role is to set the pace of learning, using thoughtful questioning to bring deeper issues to the surface or reframe the debate. At times, the teacher encourages role-playing, highlights key points on a flip chart or draws a diagram to track issues raised. As the group's time together draws to a close, the teacher moves toward a conclusion that leaves participants thinking deeply about the case and the leadership lessons it revealed, long after the discussion ends.

Thus unfolds a case discussion, a method of instruction used for decades at Harvard University in subjects ranging from law to business to public policy. Adapted by the Kansas Leadership Center to teach leadership, case discussion is an approach more demanding of learner involvement than traditional presentation or facilitation. Cases illuminate leadership principles and competencies and help equip learners to make progress on adaptive challenges.

In this chapter we briefly underscore the value of case studies for adult learning and set out six guidelines to help you prepare to successfully teach a case study. From there we offer advice about choosing a case and underscore some of the challenges related to this method. Finally, we provide two full case studies and two case vignettes, with teaching notes to get you started. More case studies and vignettes are available on the resource website associated with this book.

A CASE IS A COMPELLING STORY DESIGNED TO PROMPT MEANINGFUL QUESTIONS ABOUT LEADERSHIP AND DECISION-MAKING DILEMMAS.

KLC's cases focus on the challenges individuals encounter as they attempt to make progress on adaptive challenges. These stories generally are told in a narrative style like a short story or a film, complete with plot twists and turns. The best cases draw readers into an alternate reality; the readers start to feel like a part of the situation and to consider another's choices as if they were their own. Created through hours of interviews and research, these cases generally are told from the perspective of one or two protagonists who provide a detailed account of the problems they faced in attempting to exercise leadership. Most of the cases feature two or three sections ending with cliffhangers, which withhold the outcomes and leave participants with the responsibility for making judgments about what issues to consider and what actions to take.

Unlike a lecture, where an instructor imparts the material directly to students, a case discussion places responsibility for the direction and depth of learning on the group. The idea behind the case method is that discussion-centered learning invites participants to interact with, reinterpret and internalize material more effectively than other methods alone. It rests on a belief Harvard Business School Professor Charles Gragg espoused decades ago in support of the case method: "because wisdom can't be told." In the context of KLC, the case method supports a broader and deeper understanding of leadership principles and competencies.

Cases require learners to confront difficult, complex problems that have no single, obvious solution. A practice field for leadership, cases simulate the intensity of real-life decision making within the friendly confines of a learning group.

THEY ALSO HELP INDIVIDUALS AND TEAMS DEVELOP THEIR OWN LEADERSHIP AND DECISION-MAKING CAPACITIES.

Case teaching is interactive and learner-centered. Learners engage with the material, with you the teacher and with each other. They explore a problem and work to reach a joint resolution. From this conversation, learners develop their own way of understanding a case, and they begin to connect its events to their own situations and see that the leadership competencies that characters use (or fail to use) to make progress have applications in their lives outside the classroom.

Preparing and Teaching Your Case

In contrast to a traditional lecture, with the case method you surrender some of your authority in exchange for the possibility of a more challenging, rewarding dialogue. The method requires conscientious preparation in advance, including establishing a clear purpose to guide the work. Your role is as a facilitator and provocateur who is engaged throughout the process, making observations, interpreting what is going on and intervening to advance the discussion toward a learning goal.

Teaching a case means entering the classroom without much in the way of a step-by-step process to follow. Each story is different, as is each group of learners, which makes teaching cases both exciting and risky. The six guidelines listed below will help you as you work to master the art of teaching a case study well.

1. Establish a Purpose

In preparing to teach a case, your first step is to establish a purpose for teaching it. Often your purpose is to help participants understand a certain leadership competency well enough to apply it to their own situation. Deciding upon the purpose and relevance of the case you have chosen allows you to focus the discussion and avoid a meandering dialogue that raises interesting points but leads to no particular learning about leadership.

Embedded within the text of every meaningful case study is an identifiable set of issues or questions with possibility for wide application. For example, a case study about two nonprofits in Salina, Kansas, that are attempting a merger prompts participants to decide how the key players should act, yet it also brings to the surface rich conversation about the barriers or risks that prevent any two groups, in any context, from fully collaborating. It is this surfacing of broader issues that makes a discussion meaningful and relevant to all participants.

Teaching notes, which provide an outline for leading a discussion of the case, accompany all KLC cases. Each set of teaching notes lists a series of questions to help launch and sustain discussion as it works toward a purposeful conclusion. These materials should serve only as guides; there is no substitute for your good judgment. As you begin working with a new case, ask yourself: "What compelling leadership dilemmas does this case raise for my audience?" As you practice teaching, formulate your own approach to each case based on your answer to that question.

2. Raise Powerful Questions

Provocative questions are the lifeblood of successful case teaching. The best questions are open-ended (requiring more than a simple yes or no, right or wrong response), invite discussion and disagreement, and serve as catalysts for learners to formulate their own analyses and settle on their own conclusions. Try to prepare just three questions per section to provide structure for the discussion, but be ready to ask a number of follow-up questions, usually unscripted, to build off learner responses. Follow-up questions probe more deeply into participants' thinking, compelling them to reconsider their initial reactions or examine the situation differently.

AS YOU BEGIN WORKING WITH A NEW CASE, ASK YOURSELF:

"What compelling leadership dilemmas does this case raise for my audience?"

Sometimes it might be extremely useful to ask a question that compels learners to take a definitive stand, such as, "Was this an act of leadership or an act of cowardice?" or "Is the protagonist succeeding or failing at leadership?" This tactic helps learners move off the fence, taking more ownership in the discussion, and it helps the teacher clearly surface multiple interpretations.

Keep in mind that there are no black-and-white solutions in a leadership case. It's more about how your learners use your questions to explore leadership competencies as a blueprint for thinking adaptively. Help participants search for their own answers to a case.

YOUR JOB AS A CASE TEACHER IS TO CONSCIOUSLY CHOOSE
WHICH RESPONSES TO EXPLORE, CHALLENGE, ELEVATE OR REDIRECT,
*while keeping in mind your established
purpose for teaching the case.*

Guide them away from re-creating decisions they think protagonists might have made. This does not mean that all observations are equally relevant or serve to further the discussion to the same extent.

3. Lead as You Teach

Case teaching forces you to skillfully use the same competencies required to exercise leadership. As a case teacher, you'll certainly thrive on classroom conversation about the case, making interpretations based on those observations and intervening, in the moment, based on whatever information you have at your disposal. Yet case teaching also means ascending to the balcony from time to time, observing the effects of your interventions and adjusting your behavior accordingly. Choose actions that spur learners to get involved and to engage in the case discussion at the same level as you do.

You can almost never go wrong in following a few basic strategic moves, described in the following paragraphs, when teaching a case. When things get heated or you start to feel in doubt, these options can help reorient you to your purpose of teaching leadership. Many of the basics outlined in Chapter 1 related to Case-in-Point also apply, provided you keep in mind the differences between the two methods.

Exploring the purposes and objectives of the case's characters often will be one of the first areas you will explore with learners. You will also ask the group to make observations about the characters' behavior and actions.

Individual characters, though, usually represent groups much larger than themselves. Every leadership case contains factions, and spurring learners to identify factions in the case and excavate the loyalties, values and potential losses that the factions might be facing (or perceive they are facing) is usually crucial. Having those issues on the table creates the opportunity for the group to search for common interests among the factions as the discussion winds on.

Learners will naturally look to explain the behavior of characters through interpretations. Part of your job as a teacher will be to help learners explore multiple interpretations of the actions in the case. Encourage them to get beyond nice, convenient stories to explore systemic controversies and the clashing of values. Be on the lookout for uncomfortable or unpopular viewpoints to emerge along the way. Make sure learners spend some time struggling with those viewpoints, because that is often where the most learning lies.

At times, learners will struggle to produce multiple interpretations of a text, particularly if they share an ideology or set of core values. The controversies and clashing of values embedded in the case might not be obvious if everyone in the group holds similar political leanings and the protagonist represents the opposing viewpoint. This presents an opportunity for you to invite the group to explore its own blind spots by asking, "What is making it so hard for us to explore different interpretations?"

Throughout the case discussion, you will also have to elicit discussion about the distinctions between leadership and authority and the

FIGURE 17:

Key Case Teaching Moves

- Compel participants to consider unpopular viewpoints and interpretations.

- Get to the purpose of the case's characters.

- When in doubt, return to the basics of observations and interpretations (described in detail in the chapter on Case-in-Point).

- Prompt the group to generate observations (What did characters do?).

- Encourage multiple interpretations of actions.

- Help learners shift to tougher, systemic interpretations that invite conflict.

- Identify factions and their loyalties, values and potential losses.

- Search for common interests among factions.

- Consider how perspectives of each character change as the story progresses.

- Elicit discussion about the distinctions between leadership and authority.

differences between adaptive challenges and technical problems. What should be clear in the abstract often becomes blurred in reality, and treating adaptive challenges as technical problems and falling back on authority when leadership is required are common mistakes that derail progress, in real life as well as in case studies.

4. Move Between the Balcony and the Dance Floor

Although knowing these key case teaching moves is useful, you also must stay in discovery mode while teaching, letting each group discover its own interpretations and responding in the moment with fresh follow-up questions.

As you teach, keep asking yourself questions. Is the temperature in the room too low to produce a fruitful discussion? Are there signs that the level of conflict is increasing too rapidly for some? Are people uncomfortable with the direction the discussion is taking? This internal questioning of yourself will help you better position yourself to intervene effectively.

To be a great case teacher, you must constantly observe and interpret the group's interactions to understand what is going on in the room. Watch how participants respond to whoever is speaking. Be curious about these responses, and make observations that provoke engagement of the larger group. For instance, you could say, "It strikes me that not everyone is in your faction. Are we missing another viewpoint here?"

Stand ready to make on-the-fly adjustments to make the discussion the most powerful and provocative learning experience possible.

Also be aware of your authority and how it helps or hinders classroom discussion. Your role carries substantial responsibility for both content and process of the case discussion. Every move you make — from recognizing one person but not another, by jotting down certain comments on the flip chart and ignoring others — will be noted by participants and can affect the quality of the discussion. Be sure you are making conscious choices and stay aware of how your interventions are received.

Use your authority as the teacher to acknowledge curious questions and encourage exploration of alternative points of view. Avoid rewarding those who provide answers that you agree with or find insightful.

Successful case teachers balance the needs of individuals and the needs of the group. For instance, imagine that during a case discussion a participant reveals a personal story about a challenge she is facing. You must quickly determine whether and how this aside presents a learning opportunity for the group. To what extent is the participant's story relevant? Will exploring it further benefit the participant? What about the group as a whole? What avenues exist for reframing the story or the discussion to fit the learning goal? If this story is not relevant, how will you move the conversation forward in another direction? You must quickly read the room, make a best guess about the fruitfulness of the opportunity and decide what direction holds most closely to the purposes of the session.

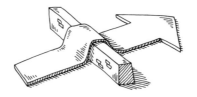

ALWAYS REMEMBER THAT IMPROVISATION LIES AT THE HEART OF CASE TEACHING.

It helps to go into the fray with a mindset that the opportunity for surprises is part of the joy of the ride, and that an important part of teaching the case method is being able to take smart risks on the fly.

5. Encourage Learners to Lead

Every case discussion presents an opportunity for teacher and learners to take risks and experience the resulting successes and failures. Engaging in experiential learning compels all participants to step outside their comfort zones. Teachers give up some control of the room by asking questions without knowing answers in advance. Participants share insights about leadership that they don't typically express aloud. Both roles have inherent risks, even in the environment of a leadership program. Considering this, teachers should temper their approach with compassion, appreciating the risks learners take and acting in ways that encourage them to speak up and act experimentally during the discussion.

Challenge learners to get close to the edge of their comfort zones while remaining respectful of the social contract that exists between teachers and learners. Meanwhile, be aware of your own tendencies and triggers, taking care to manage yourself in ways that further the discussion rather than become an impediment. For instance, if you are used to lecturing in a college classroom, you might be more comfortable presenting than asking questions and going with the flow of the group. Good self-management helps teachers recognize such a preference, which is the first step in finding ways to work around it.

6. Turn the Tables

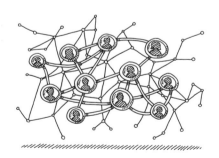

The group dynamics inherent in a case discussion mirror the ways in which important decisions get made.

Learners are confronted with a shared problem in much the same way that a community, company, city council, board of directors, executive team or legislative panel might be compelled to address a tough challenge. Successful case teaching involves turning the tables on participants to help them understand how the case relates to their own dilemmas. Executing this shift provides payoff for participants.

The goal for any teacher should be to leave learners stimulated and thinking deeply about the issues raised by a case. Some might feel confused or disoriented, because deep learning often comes with a period of disequilibrium. The teacher should resist the urge to neatly wrap up the case, an approach that undermines the idea that there is no single correct solution to the case. The teacher can assist group members by reflecting insights in their own words, or asking at the end what they are thinking about as a result of the case. Marty Linsky says it may be best to conclude by saying nothing at all, save praising the group for a good conversation.

At heart, it is the unpredictability of case teaching that makes the method both interesting and challenging. In a good case discussion, learners gain insight and examine their own behavior in a new light. Cases can be powerful vehicles for learning about leadership. Yet even the richest, most thought-provoking texts depend on the talents of the teacher to bring them to life. Those who do it effectively share control of the room with learners, acknowledge that they do not know all the right answers and assume the risks of improvising without a detailed script.

We approach case teaching as adaptive work. No formula or recipe will guarantee success, and there can be no predetermined outcome. One sign of a good discussion is that conversation among learners continues well after the session has ended. It's a signal that they have picked up something from the dialogue they can carry forward and apply in their own lives.

That's important, because the case method provides opportunities for learners to prepare themselves to deal with the challenges that come with exercising leadership, building a bridge between leadership theory and practical, everyday realities.

Choosing a Case

Now that you understand more about the case method, here are some thoughts to help you choose the first case you will present to a group. The quickest route is to choose your case based on the leadership principles and competencies you want to explore in a given program or session. Certain cases highlight specific concepts better than others; see the accompanying teaching notes for clues. Likewise, conversations with mentors and colleagues are useful for determining which case to teach and what lessons to highlight with it. Consider all of the issues at play in your group and what would be most helpful for its members to learn.

Take into account the group members and their distinctive backgrounds and interests. Different cases illustrate leadership dilemmas within different contexts. Some cases focus on individual acts of leadership. Others emphasize quandaries facing communities or teams. Don't feel that you always have to use a KLC case or purchase one from the Harvard University Press or other outlets. Newspaper articles, book chapters, novels, short stories or even a page from your company's website can serve as the text for a case teaching session. Choose carefully, keeping your learning goal in mind.

Remember that in leadership cases, it's not necessary for group members to be familiar with a case's facts, circumstances or contexts in advance. When they have too much firsthand knowledge, or if the issue hits too close to home, it can diminish the quality of a case discussion. Sometimes, the more learners know about the facts of the case, the more they get sidetracked from talking about leadership. Likewise, when too many people know the real-life outcome of the case, the discussion lacks the element of surprise that makes case teaching so much fun for anyone with a flair for the dramatic.

Your own strong understanding of leadership principles and competencies will help you decide which cases to choose and which issues to highlight. Also consider the best place for a case in the timeline of your program. Cases provide a good platform to help participants broaden and deepen their understanding of leadership, and they are a good jumping-off point to applying leadership competencies to challenges back home or at the office. Having used the case to tune up their skills, learners leave a session ready to apply similar techniques to their own leadership challenges.

Special Challenges and Pitfalls
Unfamiliar Audiences

Case studies can be great for introducing the leadership framework to new audiences, or for orienting groups to thinking about leadership issues without referring to the competencies.

When you are teaching an unfamiliar audience, we have found the following approach to be effective.

1. Spend a few minutes helping learners identify a leadership challenge they are currently facing, which gives them something in their own lives to relate to the case study they will be discussing.

2. Ask them to write the answers to the following questions: What is your purpose? Who are the factions? What are the barriers to your progress?

3. Ask them to share their responses with a partner.

4. Throughout the case teaching, prompt them to juxtapose the ideas surfacing in the case with their own challenge.

5. At the end of the case discussion, ask them to identify key lessons about leadership that came to them during the case.

6. Have them discuss with a partner how those key lessons might come into play with their personal challenge.

Debating the Facts

It's not unusual for learners to be somewhat familiar with the stories or individuals featured in a case study. Sometimes those with firsthand information about a case dispute the facts in the text rather than discussing the leadership questions the case raises. Other participants might defer to those who seem to know more background than what is presented in the case. The teacher then needs to make conscious choices to refocus the discussion on leadership. We suggest setting a ground rule in advance that participants work with the case as presented and not bring in outside factual knowledge about the story. Make sure you hold everyone in the group accountable to that agreement.

When case discussions get off track in a situation like this, you can often refocus the discussion without signaling that a comment is out of bounds. One response is to ask a participant challenging the material in a case, "What is it about the writer's viewpoint that bothers you?" or "How would you be forced to change the story you tell yourself about this situation if what is portrayed in the case were true?" These questions refocus the discussion on the case as presented without putting the commenter on the defensive. If skillfully executed, the intervention may offer fruitful avenues for digging deeper into the case.

Case Vignettes: A Focused, Flexible Option

Case studies represent a powerful tool for learning about leadership, but full-length cases aren't the right choice for every leadership learning opportunity. That's why the KLC has created a second genre of case study, a very short, extremely focused option — the "case vignette" — that will allow you to bring the power of cases into more settings, more effectively and more often.

Adapted from multi section KLC leadership cases, vignettes provide a glimpse into a leadership challenge. They fit on a single page and take no more than a minute or so to read. They tend to focus on the decision-making dilemmas of a single protagonist and are completely open-ended because there is no epilogue to resolve the story.

Because they are so concise, vignettes work best for provoking short, intense discussions, generally no longer than an hour and often as short as 20 to 30 minutes. Vignettes are specifically designed to facilitate a discussion about a single KLC principle, competency or competency sub-point, although teachers might use them more broadly at their own discretion.

The same basic approaches used to teach full-length KLC cases can be applied to vignettes. Teachers generally prepare a short list of open-ended questions and help focus the discussion with follow-up questions.

One advantage of case vignettes is they are flexible and lend themselves to a variety of different exercises and approaches. The applications for case vignettes can be as wide-ranging as you can imagine. Some teachers will use case vignettes as a starting place for a compact, focused case study discussion.

Because a case vignette contains far less detail than a full-length KLC case study, participants have greater responsibility to fill in the blanks during the discussion. The dialogue often requires them to make interpretations on the basis of sparse data. Giving participants permission and encouragement to make the best educated guesses they can with the information they have is an important aspect of the exercise.

The vignettes can also be useful as a launching pad for Case-in-Point. They provide an excellent way for a teacher to create the conditions necessary to use the discussion group as a case study. Once the group's dynamics emerge, the teacher can shift the discussion away from the vignette itself and focus on what the interventions and interactions of participants in the room illuminate about the challenges of exercising leadership.

Another way to create a shorter version of a case is to focus on only one or two parts of a case (often Part A only). If you do this, people will want closure, so be sure to have the other parts available to them if they are interested in the rest of the story.

Real-Life Dilemmas

Later in this chapter, we have included two examples of full-length case studies, as well as two case study vignettes, for you to experiment with teaching. These are among the most powerful and provocative case studies we teach; they are proven vehicles for fostering learning about leadership.

Demographic changes and the issues that arise when people of different backgrounds attempt to live, work and worship side by side represent profound leadership opportunities for organizations in many corners of the world. A three-part story about Rev. Lance Carrithers' efforts to lead his church into more intentional engagement with the Latino community in Dodge City provides an example of a widely experienced dilemma. How do you inspire people to live out their mission in the context of a new reality?

The case begins with Carrithers' realization that his predominantly white church does not reflect the changing demographics of his community, and that the community itself has subtly divided along ethnic lines as Hispanics become an ever-larger proportion of the population. The story gives learners the opportunity to explore just how risky leadership can be, and to experience for themselves that sparking meaningful change requires hard decisions, improvisation and letting go of attachment to a particular outcome.

A second full-length case highlights the perils of polarization and shows how an issue that seems straightforward can suddenly take on a life of its own. Mayor Laura McConwell thinks she understands her community's priorities, but her blind spots are revealed when the Mission City Council discusses a novel approach to funding infrastructure improvements to reinvigorate the aging suburb.

The council's ideas prompt a furor that extends far beyond her city's borders, and McConwell must decide how she'll engage with critics and keep her community focused on creating a better future. In an era where shouting at, rather than engaging with, people is too often what passes for debate, this case requires learners to make decisions about how to handle the discord that erupts when one group's idea of progress is an outrage to another.

Belief in a project alone isn't enough to bring it to reality. Crys Wood cares deeply about bringing a new, safer pool to Derby, a prosperous suburb where she had lived for about a decade, but roadblocks pop up at every turn. The first sample case vignette engages learners in exploring how Wood can best manage herself and avoid becoming a barrier to her own dreams of progress.

Another challenge of leadership is making sure you consciously advance your big-picture goal, even when potential distractions prove seductive. In the second example of a case vignette, David Toland returns from Washington, D.C., to his hometown in southeast Kansas, excited about taking the reins of a fledgling organization seeking to help reverse the county's decline. When he's unexpectedly presented with another opportunity to make a difference, he must decide if it's worth stepping up and taking a risk that could affect how he is perceived in his new job.

These cases are just a few examples from KLC's case library, which contains more than 16 full-length cases and a dozen vignettes based on longer-form case studies. The stories range from a doctor's efforts to foster a stable health system in a rural community to a group trying to create a sustainable young professionals organization. Each case was developed through meticulous research and in-person interviews and specifically tailored to bring leadership principles and competencies to life. Each one comes with teaching notes designed to help you decide which case works best to achieve your teaching goals.

All cases and case vignettes are available to purchasers of this book online at *www.kansasleadershipcenter.org/TLresources*.

As you begin to practice facilitating the cases available from KLC, you will want to periodically revisit the preceding introduction to teaching the case method and the six considerations for preparing and teaching a case. We believe these materials will leave you well equipped to create deep learning experiences for anyone striving to lead more effectively.

KLC LEADERSHIP
CASE SERIES

Dodge City's First United Methodist Church and Latino Ministry

Dodge City's First United Methodist Church and Latino Ministry

Part A

The changes occurring in southwest Kansas didn't come as a complete surprise to the Rev. Lance Carrithers when he became pastor of Dodge City's First United Methodist Church. An animated, sizable man in his 40s with a rich voice and a touch of gray hair, Carrithers had once managed a radio station and sold real estate before making a sudden career change 15 years ago. It was then that he answered a call to ministry, graduating from Saint Paul School of Theology in Kansas City.

Appointed by the Kansas West Annual Conference's bishop and his cabinet, Carrithers would be up for review in his post on an annual basis. He did not know how long he would stay in Dodge City. But pastors at First UMC tended to sustain long appointments, and he thought he might enjoy staying for a similar tenure. Carrithers' immediate predecessor had stayed seven years, and the pastor before him had remained for a decade. The church's main outreach ministries involved marketing the congregation as a "community of joy," and it sought growth as a mainline Protestant church.

Although he grew up two hours west of Dodge City, Carrithers had been working in churches located mostly near Interstate 135 in central Kansas. He had been aware that the Hispanic population in southwest Kansas' three largest counties, including his new home of Ford County, had been growing significantly. However, it wasn't until after he, his wife, Kristi, and their two teenage daughters moved to Dodge City that he realized just how significantly his congregation would be affected by that trend.

"Very quickly within that first year that I was here, it occurred to me that who this church had been, could not be what would direct us in the future," Carrithers said.

A wind-whipped city of nearly 26,000 perched on the High Plains, Dodge City extends out from a series of hills rolling above the parched bed of the Arkansas River. Founded in the 1870s as a shipping hub for longhorn cattle, Dodge City may be the state's most famous municipality. Not only is it historically linked with famous frontier lawmen Bat Masterson and Wyatt Earp, but the once rowdy cowtown also served as the setting of Western-themed entertainment programs, including "Gunsmoke." Home to the Boot Hill Museum, the city's Western heritage has remained a significant part of its identity and continued to be a draw for tourists even beyond the peak of Hollywood-inspired Wild West tourism.

Latinos — a term describing those who trace their origin to a Spanish-speaking culture or Latin America — had lived in Dodge City for decades; at one point, many were railroad workers clustered in the southern part of town. Yet for most of its history, the vast majority of the city's residents were the white descendants of Northern Europeans. That began to change in the 1980s, when the Excel Corporation opened up one of the world's largest beef-packing plants on the city's eastern edge, according to Jim Sherer, a city commissioner and a member of First UMC since the mid-1960s. That large operation, along with another Dodge City beef-packing plant, began to alter the city's ethnic makeup by drawing significant numbers of immigrant workers hailing from Asia, Mexico and Central America.

Nearly two decades later, Dodge City became a "majority minority" community where Hispanics made up more than half of the city's population and non-Hispanic whites were a minority. Within the public school system, nearly two-thirds of the students were Hispanics. The increase in population brought Latino-owned businesses to many of the historic brick buildings lining downtown. Stores there sold everything from cleated shoes for soccer to dresses for Quinceañera parties, a traditional coming-of-age ceremony in Latin American countries for girls turning age 15. Shoppers entering Wal-Mart from the often crammed parking lot found themselves greeted by signs in both Spanish and English.

Yet there were signs that Hispanic and non-Hispanic white residents often operated as two very distinct communities within the same city. Although a new Catholic cathedral drew both English and Spanish-speaking parishioners, many of the other churches conducting services in Dodge City were either predominantly Latino or mostly white. Meanwhile, inside the community's political structure, Hispanics remained vastly underrepresented in proportion to their numbers. When Carrithers came on board at First UMC, no Latinos were serving in any posts on the city commission, county commission or school board.

Nestled near neighborhoods of well-kept ranch houses in the north-central part of the city, First UMC was an imposing, 1960s-era building with an expansive buffalo grass front lawn. Its members, generally those from middle to upper-middle class backgrounds, had long played a prominent role in Dodge City's civic life.

In 1981, the church had 1,956 members and drew an average of 507 people to services each week. It counted so many business executives and political leaders among its attendees that "there were those that said First United Methodist Church ran Dodge City," said Duane Ross, a member of the church since the mid-'70s and publisher of The High Plains Journal, a regional weekly agricultural news magazine. According to Sherer, the church's mostly white membership typically included professionals ranging from educators to ranchers to agribusiness executives.

However, Carrithers realized that First UMC couldn't count on pulling its membership from the same segments of the community on which it had traditionally depended. Weekly attendance at the church's three services — traditional, contemporary and family worship — was down to an average of 400 people. Economic changes, including the trend of consolidation in agriculture, had been thinning the ranks of professionals and entrepreneurs in Dodge City.

At the same time, Carrithers could see that Dodge City's population of workers in the blue collar sector, particularly Hispanic laborers, was increasing rapidly. These workers tended to be more mobile than Dodge City workers of the past, following new job opportunities to other communities as they emerged. Although a small number of Hispanics already belonged to First UMC, mostly second- or third-generation residents of Dodge City, it was distressing to Carrithers that the city's population trends weren't being better reflected in his church's attendance and membership.

"If we were going to be a church, in my mind, that had a future, we had to find a way that we were going to better reflect who the community is today," Carrithers said.

The church already offered a regular bilingual service, which featured simultaneous translation of a sermon from English to Spanish. But participation in that service numbered fewer than a dozen people, nearly all of whom also spoke English. Attendance and enthusiasm for the service was in decline, and it would end within about a year of Carrithers becoming pastor. That left the church without any intentional ministry efforts that might appeal to Latinos who mostly spoke Spanish. Despite that, Carrithers still talked from the pulpit at regular intervals about the need for the church to be a welcoming congregation and better reflect the "whole community."

It was later that year that the pastor of a tiny Spanish-speaking congregation and two of his deacons, Benjamin Ruiz and Sergio Madriles, came to visit Carrithers in his office. The three men had heard that Carrithers might be able to help with a problem their church of about 20 people was having. The group met in a rented building in the southern part of town, and it was struggling to keep up with the rent and utilities for the drafty, leaky structure. When he heard of the Spanish-speaking congregation's predicament, Carrithers offered them the opportunity to use, free of charge, a cozy chapel on the west side of the church's building, a room that was used only sporadically by the congregation.

"They had been told that I might be able to help them, and I just simply said, 'yes,'" Carrithers said.

Soon after, the Spanish-speaking group began meeting each week, starting on Fridays or Saturdays, then later on Sundays, inside First UMC's chapel, which was separated from the rest of the church by a long hallway. The group's worship services, which featured a small band led by the pastor and his musically talented family, tended to be quite expressive in nature, a style that Carrithers said seemed closer to a Pentecostal service than what would be typical in a more staid United Methodist church. The small group's services continued for several months until the pastor left for a speaking and preaching revival engagement in New Mexico and decided not to return.

The pastor sent his wife to inform Carrithers that he had been called to serve elsewhere and wouldn't be coming back. She turned in the keys to the chapel, collected the drums, guitars, songbooks and other items being used by the group and took them with her. What Carrithers didn't know at the time, however, was that the pastor hadn't contacted the congregation and informed it of his decision. In addition, the group's members also believed that the instruments and other materials that had been removed actually belonged to the congregation.

Deacon Ruiz, a broad-shouldered mechanic in his late 30s with a mustache, said it took the church about a week to even realize that its pastor was gone. It wasn't until the group gathered for a service and the pastor didn't show up that they realized something was wrong. When the pastor failed to return the next week, Ruiz, his wife, Dolores, and Deacon Madriles began talking about what they should do. After losing both their pastor and all their worship materials, they didn't think they would be able to continue meeting inside the church's chapel.

The deacons then made a return visit to Carrithers' office, where, with the help of an interpreter, they explained the situation. As they talked, Carrithers said the group appeared forlorn but still thanked Carrithers for the help he had provided. Ruiz said they told Carrithers that their congregation's pastor had "practically abandoned" them and that, as a result, the group had decided to disband.

"It seemed like the easier thing would be for everybody to go their separate ways and find their own church," Ruiz said through an interpreter.

Dodge City's First United Methodist Church and Latino Ministry

Part B

Carrithers felt bad about the group's situation and wanted to do something to help. Although the members of the small, Spanish-speaking congregation were telling him that they wouldn't be meeting in the chapel anymore, he didn't think that the absence of a pastor should keep them from continuing to worship. So, Carrithers asked them if they wanted to still conduct services at the chapel.

"They kind of looked back like, 'You mean we can?'" Carrithers said.

He went on to tell them that the building still would be theirs to use, whether they wanted to come and pray, read scripture, lead worship or sing together.

"Whatever you can do," Carrithers said. "You're still welcome to the building. You don't have to have a pastor to have the building."

Ruiz said he was surprised by Carrithers' response, and the group was pleased to have the opportunity to continue meeting. However, Carrithers did not raise the possibility of the group becoming a formal part of First UMC. While he possessed the sole authority as a United Methodist pastor to invite the families to become members of his church, Carrithers said he did not think about extending them such an invitation.

"I had an opinion that because they had a very expressive style of worship and leaned a little bit toward the Pentecostal style of expression," Carrithers said, "they probably were not Methodist mainline folk."

Reassured that they were still allowed to meet inside the chapel, the group, essentially portions of three families, resumed worship each week. Without a pastoral authority leading them, the group's services didn't have much form or function to them at first, Carrithers said. But slowly, the group began to become more comfortable leading its own services, with Madriles beginning to preach and Ruiz delivering the liturgies. The group's presence inside the church was noticed by some at First UMC, including one man who wanted to know from Carrithers who the group was and whether its members were undocumented immigrants.

Later that year, in the fall, Carrithers received a phone call from Sergio Tristan, the new coordinator of Hispanic ministries for the Kansas West Conference of the United Methodist Church. A native of a small coal mining town in northern Mexico, the personable Tristan, in his early 50s, had come to the U.S. in 1981 and earned a master of divinity. He spoke both Spanish and English. His job was to help bolster Hispanic ministry efforts in the conference, headquartered in Wichita, which included 375 churches spanning the western two-thirds of the state. Carrithers said that although the conference had employed other Hispanic ministry coordinators previously, he rarely saw much of them. But Tristan, who had just started working that September, seemed eager to be engaged and wanted to know what was "happening with Hispanics out in Dodge City," Carrithers said.

"Well, it's interesting that you should ask that," Carrithers recalls telling Tristan, "because, well, we have this little group of people. They're not United Methodists, but they're here, they're worshiping and I wish there was some way we could be supportive of them. ... He said, 'Would you like me to come and talk with them?' I said, 'Absolutely, come out.'"

Days later, Tristan made the three-hour trip from Wichita to Dodge City to meet with the Spanish-speaking congregation. During the course of their talk, he asked them what they wanted and needed to be successful. Ruiz said his group was grateful for the opportunity to talk with Tristan and the care and attention he was paying to them and their needs.

Tristan "talked with us and really supported us, asking us: What were our dreams and goals? What did we want to get in the church and ministry? And we really felt supported," Ruiz said.

As the conversation continued, Tristan asked the group if they wanted to become part of the United Methodist denomination. He told them that becoming members of the church would provide them with advantages that they would not have if they continued being an independent congregation that simply utilized unused space in the church.

"If you join the church, you will have more support," Tristan told them.

Although they knew very little about the United Methodist Church, its doctrine or traditions, when Tristan brought up the idea of membership, the group's congregants said that, yes, they would like to join.

Dodge City's First United Methodist Church and Latino Ministry

Part C

Although he initially didn't consider that members of the Spanish-speaking congregation might want to join his church, Carrithers was delighted to hear that they desired to become United Methodists. The process began quickly, with Tristan giving the group's adults a number of initial membership lessons in Spanish. Later, a lay member of First UMC from a prominent Hispanic family in Dodge City, a man who spoke both English and Spanish fluently, helped teach another round of classes. The group, which now called itself Casa de Oracion, meaning "house of prayer" in English, continued meeting on Sundays at First UMC.

One day in December, the five adults joining the church ventured into the cavernous, triangular-shaped sanctuary at First UMC. They were there to recite their membership vows in both English and Spanish during the church's 10:55 a.m. family worship service. Carrithers intentionally had the new members stand up before the largest service and repeat their vows bilingually "as a little bit of a symbol to the congregation that this is happening — they are a part of us, and they're becoming members of the church."

The ceremony to welcome the small group of Spanish-speaking members into church significantly increased the visibility of First UMC's efforts to develop an intentional ministry to Spanish-speaking Hispanics living in Dodge City. It also, in Carrithers' mind, ratcheted up the level of the responsibility that the church had in equipping the group with what it needed to prosper, including Bibles, hymnals and Sunday school materials.

"The first assessment was that if they're members of the church, we should be providing the same sort of resources and materials that we do for any other part of the church," Carrithers said.

In addition to providing those aids, First UMC also hired a 10-hour-per-week children's ministry assistant, Maria Ferreiro, to allow the church to teach both Spanish- and English-speaking children. A consumer and mortgage lender at a Dodge City bank, the convivial Ferreiro was already a member of the church. As a native of Mexico who had lived in Dodge City for more than two decades, she spoke fluent Spanish in addition to English.

Sherer, the longtime church member and city commissioner, said he believes that most people within First UMC welcomed the Spanish-speaking families into the church. However, he acknowledges that the acceptance probably wasn't universal.

In fact, Carrithers noticed that one small group of vocal individuals appeared particularly averse to the church's efforts, resisting just about anything related to Hispanic ministry. He was concerned that this group might exert influence over a large group in the middle that was more ambivalent about the changes. Opposition rarely surfaced in a very direct way, Carrithers said, often taking the form of a churchgoer making an offhand comment to him in the hallway or after the worship service, such as: "Are we going to start speaking Spanish in this service?"

Mostly, Carrithers sensed a more cloaked resistance. Individuals seemed to be looking for an ostensibly palatable reason to avoid engagement in Hispanic ministry. He remembers one complaint which contended that Casa de Oracion attendees weren't taking very good care of the chapel and that it was "really starting to look shabby." Sometimes, when a family moved away or left the church, Carrithers had also heard it suggested that the church's efforts to include Spanish speakers was a reason for the departure.

Several months after the new members had joined, Carrithers received a call from Corey Daniel Godbey, the son of the church's director of education, Sarah, and a former associate pastor, Jim.

Entering his 30s, Godbey was tall and lean with a laid-back manner and a wide, playful smile.

He played guitar, had grown up in central and western Kansas and studied graphic design in college. For the past eight years, however, he had been working as a missionary in Mexico, where he met his wife Marina, a Mexican native. Now, Godbey told Carrithers, he and his wife, were feeling called to come to Kansas with their two young children, Caleb and Melissa. He said he was looking for a nonpastoral opportunity in which he could work in the areas of leadership development and facilitating ministry to Hispanics.

"I just started to dream of the idea of what it would look like to come back sort of where I grew up but now serving people who maybe before, when I was growing up here, weren't part of my circle of connections," Godbey said.

Carrithers hadn't been looking to hire another staff member. Having Godbey take on such a role at First UMC appealed to him, but the church lacked the money within its roughly $600,000 annual budget to bring on someone full-time in a Hispanic ministry coordinator position.

In addition, Carrithers realized that he would have to win broader support within the congregation if he wanted to hire even a part-time staff member to help with Casa de Oracion. In the past, he made many of the previous decisions to advance Hispanic ministry in the church by using his pastoral authority. But creating a new position would require approval by both the church finance committee and the staffing committee, then by the administrative council, and, finally, by First UMC's annual charge conference.

Dodge City's First United Methodist Church and Latino Ministry

Epilogue

Carrithers could sense that dedicating church resources to a coordinator of Hispanic ministry might be a thornier issue for church members to grapple with than previous changes. After all, it meant spending church funds on an enterprise that some congregants might see as exclusively benefiting the Spanish-speaking members rather than the church as a whole.

"I think everyone was OK with it as long as it was down in the chapel," Carrithers said of Casa de Oracion and the church's Hispanic ministry, "and as long as it didn't cost us."

Yet Carrithers also knew that Godbey's availability represented a significant opportunity for his church to enlist the talents of someone who could help bridge cultural divides and language barriers. Not only did Godbey speak Spanish, but the bicultural nature of his family and the deep ties he and his parents had with First UMC and western Kansas would give him a particularly unique stature within the church.

Because his church couldn't afford to hire Godbey into a full-time position on its own, Carrithers thought of an alternative. He suggested that his church could begin discussions with the Kansas West Conference about a job-sharing arrangement in which Godbey could work at First UMC for one-third of the time and spend the remaining two-thirds working across the region for the conference. Carrithers helped put Godbey in touch with Tristan and the conference; they proved amenable to the arrangement. He also embarked on the task of persuading his own congregation's church council to support the move, which would initially cost the church about $18,000 annually.

The idea met with some skepticism when it came up for discussion in the first two church committees. There were questions about devoting additional church resources to Hispanic ministry and concerns about how long it would take for Casa de Oracion to become self-sustaining by bringing in enough offerings to pay for the position on its own. But Carrithers also believed, that despite some concerns, the proposal would ultimately be approved by the church's larger administrative council and, finally, at the congregation's annual meeting, the charge conference.

"I had confidence that most of those objections were being dealt with by talking about them with the committees of the church before they came in front of the church council," Carrithers said.

Throughout the process, Carrithers said Godbey and his family's strong connections to the church proved influential in the willingness of church members to be accepting of the proposal. Although there were some doubts about the long-term implications of expanding ministry offerings to Spanish-speaking Hispanics, they viewed the hiring of Godbey as welcoming back one of their own. In fact, the process of approving the position ultimately proceeded smoothly at all levels, Carrithers said.

By that August, Godbey had started working for the Kansas West Conference, assisting Tristan as the new part-time associate coordinator of Hispanic ministries while working out of First UMC. Final approval of his position with the Dodge City church came a month later.

Even though he works part-time with Casa de Oracion, Godbey has made a significant difference in the group's growth and development into a stronger fellowship. Carrithers said that Godbey's presence has helped provide additional structure for the group. Weekly attendance has ranged from the 20s into the 30s, but over a two-year period about 100 different people became part of the group for at least some period of time. The group had even begun an evangelistic push to visit homes and develop personal relationships with more Latinos outside the fellowship.

"The most difficult thing is how to build a sustainable ministry," Carrithers said, because of the "transient nature of the people who are here for work and will, no doubt, move for work."

Although Godbey has been excited by what's been going on at Casa de Oracion, he also believes there's potential for the church to do much more. He and Carrithers both supported the hiring of a full-time bilingual pastor dedicated to Hispanic ministry, a position finally filled six years after Carrithers arrival in Dodge City.

"I think it's just about being faithful and consistent for a few years until we have a really strong base built," Godbey said.

One emphasis of Casa de Oracion has been developing the leadership capacity within the Spanish-speaking group by providing them with training they can use in ministry wherever they might live. Godbey has helped introduce Benjamin Ruiz, his wife, Dolores, and Sergio Madriles, among others, to leadership development opportunities that helped improve their ability to preach and lead the group. One former Casa de Oracion attendee has gone on to start a new faith group in Pratt. Ruiz said he appreciates how church authorities have encouraged him and others in the group to develop their potential.

"Some in the group, there were times that they were discouraged and wanted to do something else," Ruiz said. "But we set goals to grow as individuals and also spiritually, and I feel like we've met a lot of those goals."

Godbey's ability to communicate in both Spanish and English has also helped bridge the language barrier separating the church's English and Spanish speakers. In fact, since Godbey came on board, Carrithers said he has been able to more clearly see the emergence of a group of non-Hispanic whites within the church who support ministry efforts to Spanish-speaking Latinos. Ruiz said his group has learned a great deal from Godbey and that he greatly appreciates everything Carrithers has done to help Casa de Oracion.

"For him, any kind of language or racism, they aren't obstacles," Ruiz said of the senior pastor. "Those are things he works against. Things he helps us overcome."

While Ruiz hopes that Casa de Oracion will only grow more in the future, he doesn't know exactly how big it might become — "I don't want to limit God," he said. As a whole, he also said that English-speaking, non-Hispanic whites have been welcoming to the participants in Casa de Oracion.

"We can't say that everything is perfect," Ruiz acknowledges. "There are some people who probably don't want us there. But they are the minority — they are the small minority."

As church pastor, Carrithers had tried to augment the development of Casa de Oracion by continuing to push for changes that open First UMC's doors to Latinos, while also working to ensure that the church functions as a united congregation. The work has included small gestures, such as placing soccer goals out on the front lawn for use by youth soccer teams and other groups in the community. The church also conducts a bilingual children's time during its 10:55 service a.m., and its "Wonderful Wednesdays" evening meals are attended by members of both Casa de Oracion and the English-speaking services. For a time, church authorities also experimented with monthly bilingual services that brought Casa de Oracion participants together with one of the three English-speaking Sunday worship sessions. The endeavor seemed most successful when it involved the church's contemporary service, church authorities said.

The demands of conducting bilingual services monthly, however, threatened to be too taxing for Godbey and some of the church's musicians. As a result, Carrithers said the church pulled back from that effort. Carrithers said church authorities then started looking for ways to bring the church together "in a more genuine way" than "enforcing a bilingual service once a month." In the months after that change, the church has tried to offer special bilingual events, such as a parking lot tailgating party. While the church still needs "some regular interval of worship that's bilingual," Carrithers said, it hasn't quite found the right answer yet.

Figuring out the best ways to bring English-speaking and Spanish-speaking members together, though, is still a work in progress, said Duane Ross, now the publisher emeritus of The High Plains Journal.

"I would say we're trying to make steps that are tolerable to both sides," Ross said. "If we had to go to a service every Sunday that was bilingual, I'm afraid it would get very tedious to me."

The changes taking shape in the church remain difficult to contemplate for some, he acknowledges, particularly people who have gone to the church all of their lives. Yet Ross said that as long the church's mission is "telling about Christ to the world," he and his wife, Phyllis, are comfortable with its direction.

"If you try to visualize what our church is going look like in 10 years, for example, it's either going to have a lot of Mexican families and a lot of young people — it's going to be full and doing great things," Ross said. "Or it's going to be a bunch of us old folks left tottering around with one service, probably ... and an empty building."

Pushing the church forward in ministering to Spanish-speaking Latinos is a constant effort, Carrithers said, one that requires him and his church staff to be judicious in the decisions they make. He said they have to make sure that as they attempt to make progress, they do not push too far or too fast.

"We kind of keep a steady pressure, trying to move the congregation along," Carrithers said. "There's always this conversation of, 'oh yeah, we should do this.' But this will probably create a situation where we will spend so much time trying to mitigate pushback or whatever that causes, so that we'll lose ground. It's always a matter of, 'Can we push so much? And then, let up on it a little bit.'"

In Carrithers' eyes, such efforts are consistent with his belief that "the Kingdom of God as expressed through Jesus is a Kingdom that is inclusive of all." It's his ultimate hope that First UMC's efforts to become more representative of the community will be able to influence all of Dodge City for the better.

"We do this not just for the good of the church," Carrithers said. "Our congregation, no doubt, has some role in helping our larger community learn how to live together with one another in relationships of trust and in building community ... so that we really do care for our neighbors."

Teaching Notes: Parts A, B and C

Principle/Facilitation Angle

- Leadership is risky.

Primary Competency at Issue

- Energize Others.

Other Competencies at Issue

- Diagnose the Situation.

- Intervene Skillfully.

Issues Raised

- Leadership vs. authority

- Finding the zone of productive disequilibrium

- Doing what is needed, not what is comfortable

- Being more purposeful and intentional about interventions

- The risks of leadership are personal and professional

Summary

One of the KLC's leadership principles states that "leadership is risky." This case takes a look at those risks of leadership through the eyes of the Rev. Lance Carrithers, pastor of Dodge City's First United Methodist Church. The case provides an opportunity for participants to identify and evaluate the risks for Carrithers as he attempts to create a congregation inclusive of both English- and Spanish-speaking congregants. The situation provides a platform for participants to interpret when Carrithers is exercising authority and when he is exercising leadership; what opportunities he is taking advantage of; and what opportunities he might be missing. Teachers also should be cognizant of the potential for the case to raise issues that participants feel very passionately about and should be prepared to manage that heat in a way that enhances learning.

Part A

Discussion Questions

1. How would you diagnose the situation facing Rev. Carrithers at the end of this section? What's his purpose?

2. What competing values and loyalties are at stake in this case? What would be some less noble names that could be assigned to these values and loyalties?

3. What opportunities does Carrithers have to exercise leadership at this point? What are the risks of doing so?

Part B
Discussion Questions

1. How might Carrithers do what is necessary rather than comfortable in this situation? What could be getting in the way?

2. Do you see Carrithers exercising leadership or authority in this case? How far out on the edge is he?

Part C
Discussion Questions

1. What might English-speaking congregants be thinking in this section but not saying aloud? How does this situation look from the perspective of the Spanish speakers?

2. Whose church is it? (To what extent does it belong to Carrithers? The church council, committees and conference? The English-speaking congregants? The Spanish-speaking congregants?)

3. How might Carrithers intervene to make progress while disappointing at a rate they can handle?

KLC LEADERSHIP
CASE SERIES

Redeveloping Mission and the 'Driveway Tax' Controversy

Redeveloping Mission and the 'Driveway Tax' Controversy

Part A

The first emails from residents fearing a "driveway tax" began popping up on Laura McConwell's iPhone in late May. The term was new to McConwell, the elected mayor of Mission, a first-tier Johnson County suburb of nearly 10,000. The 47-year-old attorney quickly realized what concerned her constituents.

Mission city officials had spent a year discussing a Transportation Utility Fee (TUF) that would charge all owners of developed land in Mission for use of the city's streets. The city's 3,278 properties would be assessed a fee based on the estimated number of vehicle trips a piece of land produced each day. The charges would range from $72 a year for a single-family home to less than $1,000 a year for most commercial properties; however, big-box stores, fast-food restaurants and other high-traffic destinations would face far larger bills.

The fee's proceeds would help Mission address its deteriorating, potholed streets. For years, Mission had lacked a comprehensive maintenance plan, the effects of which were becoming clear. A street inventory taken two years earlier revealed that 58 percent of Mission's streets had a pavement condition index below 80, meaning they were in less than "very good" shape. Several were failing and in need of major rehabilitation.

With a struggling economy and declining property values threatening to crimp the city's traditional revenue sources, sales and property taxes, City Administrator Mike Scanlon brought a TUF to the council for further study. It would generate a chunk of the $1.5 million a year the city would need for a 10-year program to upgrade and extend the lifespan of Mission's streets. A portion of the revenue would also be used to invest in bus transit and urban trails infrastructure.

Although it had been used in other states, the charge would be the first of its kind in Kansas and the car-oriented suburbs of Kansas City. The novelty of the concept had prompted a front-page story in The Kansas City Star newspaper only a few days earlier. In explaining the idea, the reporter suggested that readers "imagine paying for the number of times you're expected to pull out of your driveway."

Working from her family's one-story law office, a side street away from Johnson Drive, Mission's main thoroughfare, McConwell's emails informed her the issue had hit talk radio, too. Shows on several Kansas City area stations had been talking about the fee, and it was being criticized on the air as an example of government excess.

"Talk radio picked it up within a day or two and started calling it a 'driveway tax,'" McConwell said. "They started talking about how people would be charged to have driveways in the City of Mission, which was completely not true."

McConwell, who had won a new four-year term that spring, had deep roots in the area. A sandy-haired mother and stepmother, she had joined the City Council 10 years ago and was elected council president a year later. She won it when the mayor, Sylvester Powell, Jr., broke a 4-4 tie between her and Councilman John Weber by flipping a coin. When Powell died, McConwell was next in the line for the agenda-setting post, which could break ties or veto action by the eight-member council.

The council McConwell inherited had been divided over the hands-on Powell, who had run the city for more than 25 years. His legacy lived on in the form of the large, striking community center that he had championed. The building bearing his name had been expanded through a quarter-cent sales tax, set to expire the next year, and depended on a subsidy of $850,000 each year from the city's general fund to operate.

As the new mayor, McConwell led a community visioning effort. She believed it was important because Mission was an "old community," surrounded on all sides by other cities and fully built out over its 2.7 square miles. A historic stopping point for wagons on the Santa Fe Trail, Mission grew from a small town after World War II, when young families flocked to the area. Modest ranch and split-level homes lined the city's tree-canopied blocks. Mission's population included a sizable contingent of senior citizens, some of whom had lived there for decades, as well as younger professionals drawn to its affordable housing.

Home to bigger stores such as Target, a cluster of small businesses lining the four-lane Johnson Drive gave the suburb a smaller-city feel. A large vacant lot sat on the city's eastern edge near Johnson Drive, Roe Avenue and Shawnee Mission Parkway. The Mission Center Mall had stood there until being razed four years ago. A mixed-use development slated to include an aquarium, retail shops and condos was supposed to replace it. But a difficult economy had stalled The Gateway, the linchpin in a master plan to reinvent Mission's commercial district.

McConwell said many people living, working, owning businesses or shopping in Mission envisioned it becoming a more walkable community, with greater connectivity between neighborhoods and the Johnson Drive business district. They also sought more green space to break up expanses of pavement and to repair the streets, which had long taken a back seat to other priorities. Residents also wanted a "thumbprint" on the city's future look rather than the haphazard growth of years past, she said.

"One of the big things of consensus was that we didn't want redevelopment to happen to us the way that development had," McConwell said.

That vision put officials on a path to promoting higher-density redevelopment in Mission, but some citizens and small business owners, many of whom lived near but not in Mission, were not on board. They tended to be particularly upset about the rebuilding of a portion of Johnson Drive, the end result of a project to remove $51 million in property from a floodplain. A quarter-mile stretch of the four-lane road was changed to three lanes with a center turn lane. The intent was to create safer conditions for pedestrians and traffic, but businesses worried it would impede traffic flow.

Similar reconfigurations were slated for Nall and Roe avenues. The city had also built an urban trail running through the heart of the city along Rock Creek. Some critics, like Weber, a retired airline electrician, often saw the city's efforts as wasteful or frivolous. Steve Schowengerdt, the owner of a remodeling business who had recently left his council seat, said council members were good people but out of touch with the community's wishes.

"The vast majority of people, they come to the suburbs because they want a little space," said Schowengerdt. "They're pushing the high density."

McConwell believed improving the city's transportation infrastructure was critical to redeveloping Mission. She also felt the council should consider a TUF when the next budget came up for approval in August. The city already planned to conduct a couple of public meetings on the proposal in the coming months, but now that the "driveway tax" was a hot topic in and around Mission, McConwell had to decide how she would best facilitate a community dialogue about the proposal.

Redeveloping Mission and the 'Driveway Tax' Controversy

Part B

McConwell responded to the concerned emails and assured citizens they'd be kept in the loop. However, with the controversy over the "driveway tax" heating up on talk radio, McConwell felt more needed to be done. She decided to alter the format of the city's public meetings on the issue.

Before bringing a Transportation Utility Fee up for debate, she first wanted to see whether residents really desired to fix Mission's streets. She worked with Scanlon, the city administrator, to set up a pair of two-hour community meetings in June and spread the word about it to homeowners and merchant groups. Each "Transportation Needs Forum" drew about 70 people to the community center.

At the meetings, McConwell explained that well-maintained streets were just one of many important areas competing for city resources. Other needs included storm water infrastructure, the community center, parks, maintaining and expanding trail systems, the city's outdoor swimming pool, launching a downtown farmer's market and bringing City Hall into compliance with the Americans with Disabilities Act.

"I wanted them to understand all of the issues we're dealing with, and I wanted to find out whether or not people really wanted us to work on these issues," McConwell said. "Because if they don't want us to work on the roads, if they don't want us to work on the infrastructure and if they don't want us to do this and that, then we don't need to have the other meetings."

The city also released a survey allowing stakeholders to weigh in on the community's needs and street maintenance. McConwell said the citizens providing input wanted to repair the streets and believed the improvements would help attain their goal of seeing Mission redevelop.

"There were one or two people that didn't want us to fix the streets, but that was it," McConwell said. "Nobody else said 'don't fix the roads.' Even those people who told us not to fix the roads, they just questioned the timing of it."

The mayor and city staff then set up two more public meetings in August, a few days before the city was to consider its proposed budget. These forums would allow city officials to outline street-repair funding options for the public to review and discuss. The mayor publicized the session in a special edition of her newsletter.

About 50 people showed up for each Transportation Funding Forum at the community center. Upon arrival, participants were divided into a half-dozen small groups to complete a "pie exercise." Each group was given a kit containing several pie slices that represented funding mechanisms available to the city. A city staff member and council member were assigned to each table to help answer questions.

To fund a street repair program over 10 years, Mission needed to generate $1.5 million each year from mostly local revenue sources. The city expected to receive about $250,000 each year from the state and highway funding. Participants would discuss the situation and decide where the remaining $1.25 million would come from on an annual basis. Their choices included: (1) sales taxes; (2) property taxes; (3) TUFs; (4) special assessments directly to property owners abutting a street; and (5) cuts in city services.

Each group's preferred combinations varied significantly. Most tables favored obtaining about one-half to one-third of the aid for street repairs from sales taxes. Some wanted as much as half of the money to come from a TUF, others less than 10 percent. One group failed to reach any consensus at all. However, when the city officials averaged all the pies, they suggested a street program with one-third of the money from a quarter-cent sales tax, a third from a TUF and a third from a combination of property taxes, the city general fund and state and highway funds.

Jo Ella Hoye, a 26-year-old resident who attended a forum, said her group of three, which included a middle-aged man and an elderly gentleman, smoothly reached a consensus on their table's pie. A management and budget analyst in the county manager's office, Hoye also served on the downtown visioning committee. She thought a TUF was an intriguing idea going in and felt she gained from hearing the other perspectives at the meeting, even if it wasn't a huge crowd.

The TUF proved appealing to her group, she said, because it would be a dedicated source for transportation infrastructure improvements. It would also be less burdensome on businesses than raising funds from property taxes, since all properties — including churches, schools and government — would pay the fee, she said. There was also excitement that, in conjunction with road improvements, Mission could be made friendlier to walking and biking, particularly around Johnson Drive.

"They didn't limit it to filling potholes," Hoye said of city officials. "They recognized that transportation doesn't just occur in a car."

Another participant, Bill Nichols, was not impressed by the process. The 70-year-old retired photographer active in the area Tea Party movement had been seated at the same table as the mayor, city administrator, a council member and a couple of other citizens. He felt that his group hadn't come to a consensus, but one member, a nonretail business owner, reported otherwise to the full group, something Nichols brought up after the meeting. Nichols disliked the idea of a TUF. If the city was going do anything, he felt it should ask voters to pass a sales tax for the roads. He also felt like the city was spending money on unnecessary infrastructure changes — such as bike paths and reducing some street lanes — when it should be tightening its belt in a bad economy.

"It's just a mystery to me," Nichols said. "I don't understand how these people think."

About a week later, the Mission City Council took up an ordinance authorizing a TUF to collect up to $833,000 for the coming year. Three citizens, including Nichols, spoke out against the fee. The mayor and others on the council argued that it was a necessary source of road maintenance funding. Unless the city did something now, improvements would be more costly in the future, McConwell said.

The council voted 7-1 to approve the TUF, with Councilman Weber casting the lone "no" vote. Nichols was "shocked" by the council's action on the TUF and felt the earlier public meeting he had attended hadn't affected the outcome.

"In my opinion, it was a done deal," Nichols said.

The next morning, McConwell awoke at 5 a.m. to a phone call. A talk radio show wanted to record an interview with her in 20 minutes about the council's passage of the "driveway tax." McConwell realized that it would probably be far from the last media request she would be receiving in the days ahead.

Redeveloping Mission and the 'Driveway Tax' Controversy

Epilogue

Several dozen people, mostly business owners, gathered inside the dimly lit, historic Mission Theatre on Johnson Drive to express their anger and frustration. One by one, they took the microphone from Mike Scanlon, the city administrator, and pointedly questioned the council's decision to institute a Transportation Utility Fee.

The City of Mission was conducting the first of two public meetings to provide information about the TUF and how it was calculated and to explain how it would be used to pay for street improvements. For those on hand, however, it was also a chance to confront city officials over the decision that had been made.

Some in attendance questioned the process the council had used to pass the fee. A few said they hadn't known about it until after it was passed; others were upset that there was not a way for it to be brought to a vote. They also questioned the city's spending decisions, such as the narrowing of streets and building of wider sidewalks, and characterized them as bad or wasteful. They argued that the TUF would hurt Mission's economy in already tough times and drive the city into further economic decline. One mentioned the vacant lot where the Mission Center Mall used to be as evidence that the city's overall vision for redevelopment was going nowhere.

McConwell stood at the front of the room, responding to their questions, concerns and complaints in a calm but direct manner. She explained that the TUF would supply a transparent, dedicated stream of revenue for repairing Mission's streets and would be spread more evenly than a large property tax increase. She pointed out how the city could move forward with discussing a sales tax question to reduce the size of the TUF, an idea that had sprung from discussions with the public. She also emphasized that most of the residents and business owners who had attended the public forums wanted the city to focus on its infrastructure needs. She also said that Mission's redevelopment plan was taking shape and The Gateway would happen.

The exchanges didn't seem to be changing too many minds in the room, but McConwell held steady. Since the council's passage of the TUF, she had served as the city's chief representative in responding to public concerns about the "driveway tax." The new fee received widespread newspaper, radio and television coverage across the Kansas City metro area and was critically analyzed by conservative bloggers and on Fox Business News. The Kansas chapter of the National Federation of Independent Business, a small-business advocacy group, issued a statement contending that the TUF was the kind of policy that would "further stagnate and crush" economic growth in Kansas.

McConwell said she could not have anticipated the sheer amount of attention the council's action on the TUF would receive, particularly from outsiders.

"I didn't understand that — in addition to working to educate the people that lived in Mission, owned property in Mission or had businesses in Mission — we would have to educate the rest of the metropolitan area, the rest of the state and potentially the rest of the country," McConwell said.

The mayor believes much of the fuss grew from the nation's current political climate, in which many Americans are gravely concerned about government taxation and spending in the aftermath of the nation's worst recession in a half-century, the ensuing taxpayer-funded bailouts and a federal stimulus. From her perspective, much of the anger erupting has very little to do with Mission instituting a new fee to fix its streets.

"What we're getting now is more of a reaction of what's going at the federal or the state level or other issues going on in people's lives," McConwell said. "I find that out a lot. For people that are unhappy about something, I'm a safe person to come and yell at."

Furthermore, McConwell said many of the individuals most vocally upset about the TUF are the same people who have been angered by previous city decisions, such as disaffected business owners on Johnson Drive. Other critics in the community are simply embarrassed by the negative attention that Mission had been receiving. Some in Mission who do not oppose the TUF have remained quiet because they do not want to risk the ire of those who oppose it, she said.

"What we were doing on the streets was really just a continuation of what we had been working on," McConwell said. "I think some of the people that I'm not hearing from speak louder volumes to me than some of the people we have heard about." Those upset about the fee, like Beverly O'Donnell, owner of the Mission Bowl just off Johnson Drive, believe that the city council failed to adequately listen to the people on the issue. O'Donnell, an Overland Park resident whose family business has been in Mission since 1958, said she did not know anything about the TUF until after the city council had approved it. She believes the vast majority of Mission was against it and the council "snuck it in there."

"I wish every politician would listen to the people that elected them, whether it's in this situation or all over the United States," said O'Donnell, one of the speakers during the meeting at the Mission Theatre. "They just aren't listening to the people who voted them in."

By fall, McConwell was facilitating a public discussion about putting a sales-tax question on the ballot to reduce the amount needed from the city's TUF. Voters could decide whether to pass a 10-year quarter-cent sales tax to replace the expiring one that had been used for the community center expansion. The city has also begun sharing information with property owners about what they will owe; property owners who disagree with their assessments could appeal to have their land reclassified to less intense uses.

Scanlon, the city administrator, said this is a good time to try the new fee because the tax bills of many landowners are falling in conjunction with decreasing property values. He said developments eventually will be able to drive down their trip charges by sharing parking lots and promoting non car forms of transportation.

"You want to try to use these models both as a way to pay for things but also as a way to incentivize better development as you go forward," Scanlon said. "To me, part of a Transportation Utility Fee is getting people to think about how land is used and how to share parking."

In the meantime, opponents plan to continue their fight against the TUF. There's been some discussion of filing a lawsuit challenging the city's authority to institute the fee. One visible reminder that the controversy probably won't be going away soon has popped up in yards around the city: yellow political signs featuring the silhouette of a house perched behind a winding drive. The text on the placard reads: "Save Mission! Repeal the Driveway Tax."

Teaching Notes: Parts A, B and Epilogue

Principle/Facilitation Angle

- It starts with you and must engage others.

Primary Competencies at Issue

- Diagnose Situation.

- Intervene Skillfully.

- Energize Others.

Other Competencies at Issue

- Manage Self.

Objectives/Issues Raised

- Explore the challenges of helping a community explore the gap between reality and aspiration.

- Encourage careful thinking about the difference between technical and adaptive challenges.

- Provoke a shift to systemic thinking.

- Explore how to engage effectively with dissenting or discordant voices.

- Specifically raise issues related to the built environment and healthy community design.

Summary

The case explores the challenges of mobilizing a community to do difficult work related to assessing its less than ideal reality and outlining a better future. It also provides a useful training ground for distinguishing between technical and adaptive challenges. At the heart of the matter is how Laura McConwell can use not just her authority, but also her leadership, to help Mission move forward and adequately address the concerns of all of its citizens. Using provocative terms, such as "driveway tax," might prove especially useful in making this a case about the clashing of values.

Part A
Discussion Questions

1. How would you describe the adaptive challenge this case presents? Whose job is it to determine a community's future?

2. If you're Mayor McConwell, what keeps you up at night in this situation? What do you worry about, and whom do you worry about pleasing?

3. What factions can you identify in the case? What values and potential gains and losses do they have?

4. What purpose should drive McConwell in this situation? What should her community engagement strategy look like?

Part B
Discussion Questions

1. Adaptive issues usually involve change to the culture of a system. How might the long history with the late Mayor Powell in Part A be playing out in the citizen reaction occurring in Part B?

2. How might the understanding of culture cause McConwell and the city administrator to approach this work differently?

3. How trustworthy is the process that McConwell uses to facilitate a community discussion of the "driveway tax"? Is this authentic engagement or covering your backside?

Epilogue

Discussion Questions

1. Has anyone questioned our consistent use of "driveway tax" instead of "Transportation Utility Fee?" What language should we have used, and what was the impact of the terms we used?

2. How does this case relate to healthy community design challenges within your own context?

3. What would it look like in this situation to "speak from the heart"? To speak to loss?

4. How might you cross factions?

"How Do You Keep From Being a Barrier to Your Own Dreams of Progress?"

"How Do You Keep From Being a Barrier to Your Own Dreams of Progress?"

Crys Wood wants to do her part to bring a new aquatic center to Derby.

Crys Wood spent several years unsuccessfully working for a new swimming pool in Derby, a prosperous Wichita suburb of 18,000 where she had lived for more than a decade.

Derby was home to an aging municipal pool. It had been built in 1964, when the town had 7,000 residents. Wood initially worried about the safety of the pool, which had a cramped parking lot.

A spirited woman entering her 40s, Wood had a son and daughter on the local swimming club team, the Derby Dolphins. A school paraprofessional, she was outgoing but easily distracted. Heavily involved in her church, she would reference her Christian faith in conversation.

When she began working for a new pool, she called a friend on the city council, who suggested she ask the community's "godfathers" — a handful of long-prominent Derby citizens — to get behind the idea. But Wood directly raised the issue with the city council instead. The council sent her to the city's park board, which she joined for a few months. She found little interest there for building a new pool and resigned after a few months.

Later that year, Wood's involvement with the swim club gave her a new way to make progress on her goal. She found an ally in another swim club parent, an accountant named Charlie Schwarz. They formed a group of about a dozen swimming parents working on a new pool.

City officials remained skeptical about the project, which was not a top priority with other building projects going on. After the September 11 terrorist attacks, Wood questioned whether the parents group should even move forward, "in light of our current national situation." Schwarz, who had been elected the group's president, argued the group should continue pushing the city council on building a new Derby pool.

The rest of the group agreed with Schwarz. Wood went on to coin the parent group's name: Supporters of Aquatic Center, or SOAC (pronounced soak) for short. Now she would have to determine how she would be most effective at achieving her long-sought goal of bringing a new pool to Derby.

Teaching Notes

Principles Explored

- Leadership is an activity, not a position.

- Anyone can lead, anytime, anywhere.

- It starts with you and must engage others.

- It's risky.

Competency Subpoints Explored

- Know your strengths, vulnerabilities and triggers.

- Know the story others tell about you.

- Choose among competing values.

- Get used to uncertainty and conflict.

- Experiment beyond your comfort zone.

Suggested Facilitation Time

- 20–30 minutes.

Key Facilitation Questions

1. What interpretations can you make about Wood's efforts? What tough or systemic interpretations might be made?

2. What potential default behaviors might Wood be engaging in? How might others, like the city council, be responding to her?

3. What are her vulnerabilities? What strengths does she have to leverage?

4. What story is Wood telling herself about her role in this situation? What stories might others be telling about her role?

5. What competing values are on the line for Wood in this situation?

6. How might Wood experiment beyond her comfort zone to be a facilitator, rather than a barrier, to progress?

Potential Reflection Questions

1. What tendencies or default behaviors have you brought with you into the room today?

2. What stories might others here be telling about you? What stories do people who interact with you in the community tell about you?

3. To what extent have your strengths and vulnerabilities manifested themselves during this discussion? When do they show up for you?

4. To what extent have you experimented beyond your comfort zone here? What experiments could you try?

5. In what ways might you be a barrier to your own dreams of progress? How might you play a different role to help make progress in this room or in your community or organization?

"How Do You Advance Your Purpose?"

"How Do You Advance Your Purpose?"

David Toland returns to his southeast Kansas hometown to lead a nonprofit seeking to improve health in Allen County.

David Toland's roots ran deep in Allen County, a southeast county of about 13,000 people. Boyish-looking and in his early 30s, Toland was the seventh generation of his family from the area. For most of the past six years, he had lived in Washington, D.C., rising in the ranks of city government there. However, Toland and his wife recently had their first child and wanted to return to Kansas.

One night, Toland received a phone call from his childhood physician, who lived in the county seat of Iola. The doctor was the board chairman of Thrive Allen County, a two-year-old nonprofit dedicated to improving health, wellness, education and recreation conditions in the county. He wanted to see if Toland was interested in becoming the organization's first full-time director.

The outgoing Toland ultimately took the job. The task appeared daunting, because Allen County's fortunes had seemingly been waning since the end of a natural gas boom in the early 20th century. Once a rapidly industrializing home to nearly 28,000 people, Allen County had lost nearly 1 percent of its population each year. It had high rates of poverty and health issues such as low rates of physical activity and high rates of obesity, smoking and alcohol abuse. Other concerns involved the availability of medical and dental services, a lack of transportation for the needy and elderly, and few recreational venues accessible to the entire community.

But Allen County now had a special opportunity to make progress. The nonprofit that ran its hospital had been sold a few years earlier. The transaction resulted in the formation of two regional foundations, one of which provided the aid that helped local citizens launch Thrive.

Toland was excited about the "opportunity to create something and, hopefully, create it the right way, or at least what I think is the right way." But he also needed to set up the organization's first office and bring in enough grant funding to pay his salary. Plus, beyond the close-knit executive board, it was not exactly clear to him who served on the Thrive Allen County Board of Directors.

Just a few days after he moved to Allen County, though, he attended a community meeting to discuss the construction of new, centralized school buildings for the city's school district. Toland suggested the idea of constructing the project so part of it could function as a community recreation center. After speaking up, Toland found himself being asked to be chairman of a special committee, the Joint Facilities Task Force, which would study such a possibility.

He had not yet officially started his job with Thrive Allen County.

Teaching Notes

Principles Explored

- It starts with you and must engage others.

- Your purpose must be clear.

- It's risky.

Competency Subpoints Explored

- Make conscious choices.

- Hold to purpose.

- Raise the heat.

- Give the work back.

- Act experimentally.

- Speak from the heart.

Suggested Facilitation Time

- 30–45 minutes.

Key Facilitation Questions

1. How would you diagnose the situation facing Toland? What is his purpose? What interpretations and viewpoints should he be considering?

2. What options to intervene does Toland have to advance his purpose in this situation? How might he raise the heat? Give the work back? Speak from the heart?

3. What would it look like for Toland to act experimentally in this situation?

4. If you had to choose one path forward for Toland to hold to his purpose, what would it be?

Reflection Questions

1. What is your purpose here, and how well have you held to it? How has your behavior here been similar or different from how you behave in your community?

2. To what extent have you been making conscious choices while intervening in this discussion?

3. How might you have intervened differently in this room? How might you intervene differently in your community?

4. To what extent have you been willing to take higher-risk interventions, such as raising the heat, giving the work back or speaking from the heart? What are the barriers to intervening in those ways? How have those barriers manifested themselves in this room?

5. How might you act experimentally going forward (on your leadership challenge or in deploying the competencies/intervening skillfully)?

CHAPTER 3

Coaching to Make Progress on Adaptive Challenges

Coaching to Make Progress on Adaptive Challenges

In this chapter we describe what makes the KLC approach to leadership coaching unique, all the while acknowledging its grounding in the field of professional coaching. We highlight the importance of managing self in the coaching relationship and provide tools, including a coaching agreement, guidelines for navigating your first meeting with a learner, our L.E.A.D Model and a set of powerful coaching questions based on our leadership principles and competencies.

Imagine this scenario:

An organization is reeling in the wake of the unanticipated departure of its founder and CEO. The board names Eloise, a young staffer, to the Interim CEO position, directing her to take on all fiscal responsibilities and significantly reducing the portfolio of Jerry, a much older colleague. When Jerry actively resists the change in job description, Eloise comes to her leadership coach for help in understanding her predicament.

As Eloise focuses on the technical details of shifting tasks from one desk to another, her coach draws on the competency of Diagnose Situation. With Eloise's agreement that a shift in thinking would be helpful, the coach moves the conversation toward the more difficult, adaptive work at hand. Listening actively and empathetically, the coach interjects questions that move Eloise's resolve from "getting Jerry to see things my way" to exploring different perspectives on what is happening. As they talk, Eloise considers a number of interpretations of the situation, and her coach uses a mix of intuition and experience to guide the conversation through a series of thought-provoking questions:

- What outdated organizational values does Jerry's behavior represent?

- What new attitudes might help navigate these rough waters?

- Who is losing what as things change?

As the coaching conversation progresses, Eloise recognizes the degree to which her organization has been knocked out of balance by the founder's abrupt exit. She acknowledges the high level of distress and the conflicting values that provoked Jerry's stonewalling, and she starts to recognize less obvious signals of distress from other staff and board members. Realizing the complexity of the challenge she is facing, and acknowledging that the heat is too high for most people to handle, Eloise begins to consider ways to calm things down just enough for people to see things clearly. She understands that she won't be able to fix things on her own, even from her new position of authority, and that she'll need colleagues to take ownership of the inherent challenges (rather than push them back on her) and share the work required for the organization to survive.

As the coaching session comes to a close, the coach asks Eloise to observe herself in action during the next couple of weeks, reflecting in writing about her own reactions to situations and events. With that request, the coach prepares Eloise for their next conversation, which, if the coach's instincts are correct, will be built around the competency of Manage Self.

Leadership Coaching: What is It? What is Its Purpose?

This scenario provides a hint of what leadership coaching would sound like if we were to press an ear to the door of a confidential conversation between two members of a coaching partnership. The Kansas Leadership Center's approach to coaching encourages individuals to adopt an experimental approach to understanding leadership situations and supports those individuals in building the capacity to take smart risks in service of something they care about. Leadership coaches support more frequent and effective acts of leadership at all levels in businesses, organizations, institutions and communities. Because most problems facing 21st-century communities contain adaptive elements that cannot be solved by authority alone, our coaching model is designed to support anyone (from CEOs like Eloise, to staffers like Jerry, to community volunteers and elected officials) who needs to engage others more effectively on behalf of an important purpose. In practical terms, leadership coaches use skills, such as active listening and good open-ended questions, and the competencies and principles to help individuals understand challenges, set leadership goals and take action to achieve those goals. Along the way, learners learn about leadership and develop a language to help them understand what is happening in their organization or community. A good coach holds learners accountable to try new leadership behaviors and learn from the results, helps them stay engaged and optimistic when things get difficult, and makes sure that learners take the time to celebrate learning and progress. Leadership coaches challenge and support individuals (and teams) to find their voices, listen deeply to others and exercise leadership on behalf of what they care about.

The Coach's Foundation

KLC's coaching model builds on the basics of leadership and the basics of coaching. If you want to be a leadership coach, you must first exercise leadership. Put yourself out there in your organization, company and community. Try intervening in new ways that don't come naturally. You'll gain new perspectives and increase your credibility with your learners if you practice what you coach. Have a complex adaptive challenge that you are working on, ideally one at work and one as a volunteer. Experiment all the time. Try to make progress. Contribute your time and energy to helping people work together to solve seemingly intractable problems. Then, with empathy and wisdom grounded in your own experience, sit down with your learner and coach.

Begin each coaching conversation by reminding yourself that your learner is whole and complete and able to lead. Listen actively, deeply and generously. Meet learners where they are. Stay curious about how the person you are coaching defines a meaningful life and how exercising leadership contributes to that. Abandon polite conversation. Instead, share your observations, insights, interpretations, even intuition, with the learner if you think it will help. Challenge the learner to experiment with KLC's leadership behaviors. Help a learner discover new possibilities for making a difference. Be with learners and ask for their best. Model the way of leadership. That's what leadership coaching is all about.

The clearer you can be at the start of each engagement about what coaching is and what it is not, the more secure your learner will feel in sharing dreams and details with you. Make sure you know and clarify for your learner the distinctions between the following common — and often overlapping — roles.

Here are some of the things that coaching is NOT[1]:

Facilitating,

because facilitating is a process of moving a group through specific content to a desired outcome.

Mentoring,

because mentoring is imparting knowledge to another to guide him/her based on personal experiences.

Counseling,

because counseling examines how the past relates to the present, providing sympathy and empathy.

Consulting,

because consulting is gathering, assessing and evaluating information to reach a recommendation on behalf of another.

[1] These descriptions of what coaching is not were developed by Dr. Patrick Williams. Used with permission. For a more in-depth discussion of the distinctions between coaching and other sources of support see, "Border Line: Understanding the Relationship Between Therapy and Coaching," by Patrick Williams, EdD, MCC, in Choice Magazine, Volume 5, Number 3, available at *www.choice-online.com.*

Instead, leadership coaching concentrates on helping people become who they need to be and do what they need to do to successfully energize others to make progress on big challenges. Coaching is a partnership that generates an exchange of inspiration and learning between coach and learner. A successful coaching relationship starts with a strong agreement. That agreement clarifies the long-term purpose of your work together, articulating what needs to happen for the learner to find real value in the coaching relationship.

Creating a strong agreement sometimes means listening for what is not being said to discover what motivates a learner or what might get in the way of a productive coaching partnership. At KLC, learners are assigned a coach as one component of leadership development training. Some come to coaching reluctantly, already adding up the hours they've spent in the classroom and resenting the additional time required for coaching. As the coach, listen for resistance. Be ready to empathize. Acknowledge that after so much time away from work, the coaching engagement can feel like just another meeting on an already over-full calendar. Embrace this opportunity to help the learner debrief the classroom experience. Ask questions that help determine what would make your time together really useful. Then, listen actively and deeply to the answers, building on the response to begin crafting goals for your work together. Throughout the coaching engagement, keep coming back to questions about productivity and value, training the learner to set a clear agenda for each coaching session. Each time you meet, get clear direction about what would help the learner be more successful at exercising leadership.

As you craft this agreement, make it clear that you want feedback and direction about what is working in the coaching relationship and what isn't. Let the learner teach you to be a great coach. Create space for the learner to ask directly for what he or she needs from you. Respond to requests confidently. Don't take criticism personally. If a learner asks you to shift your approach or do something differently, don't be embarrassed or waste time second-guessing your coaching skills. Ask for feedback before, during and after each session. Then, take that feedback to heart and do what is necessary to increase the value of the coaching relationship.

FEEDBACK, EVEN CRITICISM, IS CAUSE FOR CELEBRATION
*because it means that a learner is taking
responsibility for the success of the relationship.*

Beginning coaches stumble when they fail to ask learners for feedback often enough. A constant back-and-forth with learners co-creates and refines your shared agenda and generates real results as the learner, with coaching from you, tries out the KLC competencies and begins to lead in a different way. Midway through your first conversation with a learner, pause and ask, "Is this helpful?" or "What can we do right now to make this coaching session even more valuable?"

At the end of each meeting or phone call, pose one or more of the following questions:

- What was most valuable about our conversation?

- What did I do that was most helpful?

- What would have been more helpful?

- What can each of us do to make our next conversation even more useful for you?

An energetic dialogue about the coaching process itself is vital in these short coaching engagements that follow a leadership development experience. If you as the coach feel stuck about how to proceed with a conversation — or if you catch yourself talking too much — share your thoughts with learners in the moment. Then ask for help getting back on the most productive track. Never be afraid to ask a learner, "Is this working for you? How can we make it better?"

Questions like these help the learner become a full partner in the coaching relationship, directing both the content and process of each meeting or call instead of allowing the coach to have authority over what happens. Encourage learners to set aside reflection time before each session, and send a reminder email before the first few sessions requesting that they share notes with you in advance.

Confidentiality: The Coach's Core Value

KLC embraces an ethic of confidentiality in the coaching relationships we sponsor. Our coaches work with learners to build and maintain a trusted container for conversation, insights and experimentation. Within that container, both coach and learner can take the risks required to foster acts of leadership. Coaches initiate a trustworthy process with each learner when they promise to maintain the strictest levels of confidentiality with all information. Our coaches obtain a clear written agreement outlining the details of confidentiality and any exceptions; for instance, KLC's coaching agreement requests a few exceptions to confidentiality for coach credentialing purposes. (Learners may choose whether or not to grant permission for those exceptions).

Coaches honor agreed-upon exceptions to confidentiality by strictly limiting conversation about learners to scheduled meetings, either with their mentor coach or with a peer group of coaches. These meetings must be for the stated purpose of mentoring, developing coaching skills and building capacity to serve coaching learners. Coaches refrain from discussing, alluding to or sharing stories about learners with anyone else, including sponsor organization staff or faculty. They should also avoid conversation about learners with fellow coaches outside confidential mentoring or peer-learning situations. Unless a coach has explicit permission from the learner, he or she never offers clues that might link an individual learner with a situation or story, even for the purposes of coach training or his or her own learning. The best way to honor learner confidentiality is — in adherence with the International Coach Federation (ICF) Code of Ethics — never tell anyone whom you are coaching, even when (as often happens in leadership programs) the list of coach and learner matches is generally available.

Confidentiality is the coach's core value. As a coach gains experience, he or she begins to embody other important values, such as curiosity, non-judgment and lack of attachment to outcome, and develops coaching skills and becomes more adept at using them to build leadership capacity in others. But coaches never lose sight of confidentiality as the foundation for everything else. They honor and protect it, knowing that breaking confidentiality loses a learner's trust, and with it the ability to make progress. And if coaches are working as part of a leadership development program, violating confidentiality seriously undermines the reputation of the sponsoring organization.

Coaching Presence: Managing Self in the Coaching Relationship

Coaching presence is at the very core of what allows you to manage yourself effectively in a coaching relationship. Presence is the ability to be fully conscious and create a spontaneous relationship with the learner, staying open, flexible and confident. As a coach, your presence is the strong personal foundation upon which you exercise leadership, taking the risks necessary to support learners in real, meaningful and productive ways. Presence supports your ability to tolerate uncertainty and conflict in civic and organizational life and in conversations with learners.

In being present for your learner,
YOU MODEL AND ENCOURAGE THAT LEARNER'S ABILITY TO REMAIN
PRESENT IN SITUATIONS THAT REQUIRE LEADERSHIP.

One measure of your capacity to manage yourself in the coaching relationship is the extent to which you bring both inner strength and empathy to each learner interaction.

Mary Beth O'Neill calls this range of capacity "Backbone and Heart."

"BACKBONE IS ABOUT SAYING WHAT YOUR POSITION IS, WHETHER IT IS POPULAR OR NOT."

"HEART IS STAYING IN A RELATIONSHIP AND REACHING OUT EVEN WHEN THAT RELATIONSHIP IS IN CONFLICT."

Developing Presence

Developing presence is an all-day, everyday effort. As you develop yourself as a leadership coach, work consciously to strengthen your presence and model it for learners. Take time to clarify your core values and the purpose of your work, making choices and adjustments to bring yourself into a state of integrity and alignment with those core values. Practice speaking from your heart and going with your gut while remaining open to the possibility that you will be wrong once in a while.

Continually assess yourself and develop the backbone required to challenge learners to step outside of their comfort zones. Of course, all the while you must nurture the heart of compassionate understanding that allows you to maintain a relationship with a learner.

Take time outside of work to learn and practice habits that support coaching presence. Develop a "presence practice" — such as meditation, centering prayer, walking or yoga — apart from your coaching interactions. Learn to listen to your body and train yourself to pay attention to your gut and your intuition. Then bring what you are practicing into your relationships by creating a short centering ritual to prepare yourself for each session.

During the coaching conversation,
STAY AWARE OF THE EBB AND FLOW OF PRESENCE
by noticing when your attention wanders and developing practices to
BRING YOURSELF BACK TO THE PRESENT MOMENT.

As you learn and practice your own techniques for being wholly present, you can begin to support learners in doing the same. Invite them to practice presence during the coaching call and suggest or teach ways for them to cultivate their own presence outside of the coaching partnership. Take time to encourage learners to listen to the wisdom of the heart and gut, and continually inquire of yourself what you need to do or practice to strengthen your own coaching backbone or open your heart even more.

The Journey to Coaching Mastery

If you want to coach people to make progress on adaptive challenges, first you need to develop your basic coaching skills, preferably by enrolling in an ICF-approved coach training program. A good training program — such as the one we offer at KLC — introduces the 11 coaching core competencies listed in Figure 18 and provides plenty of opportunities for students to practice coaching and get feedback from instructors in face-to-face and virtual coaching situations.

If you are new to the coaching role, it is also essential to engage in coaching yourself with a credentialed coach, as well as mentoring and supervision from experienced coaches who are qualified to help you develop your skills and presence.

All KLC leadership coaches complete a minimum of 33 hours of training before they begin coaching for us. Most have completed the 70 hours of training plus mentoring, supervision, practice, and the oral and written assessments required to attain the KLC Certified Leadership Coach designation. Several possess a more advanced ICF credential. In addition to our own certification, we provide professional development opportunities to encourage all of our coach team members to work toward professional credentialing through the ICF.

Coaching Tools

In the pages that follow, you will find our L.E.A.D Coaching Model, plus useful tools and coaching questions that we hope you will use in your coaching practice. We invite you to use the leadership principles and competencies as your framework, and to adapt your materials to your own situation or environment. These resources will help with coaching in a variety of settings, whether you are partnering with an elected official, school administrator, corporate or nonprofit executive, pastor, small business owner, community volunteer or any of the myriad individuals from all walks of life who wish to lead more often and more effectively.

We invite you to join us in seeking out opportunities to leverage the power of coaching to support and inspire people to experience the deep satisfaction that comes from addressing adaptive challenges in organizations and communities. KLC's use of coaching to bolster the experience of learners and further their learning has produced a track record of proven results.

COACHING SPEEDS AND SUSTAINS LEARNING
and helps individuals do the work of incorporating what they learned during a classroom or training session into their daily lives and work.

The following eleven core coaching competencies were developed to support greater understanding about the skills and approaches used within today's coaching profession as defined by the International Coach Federation

A.
{ SETTING THE FOUNDATION }

1. Meeting Ethical Guidelines and Professional Standards
2. Establishing the Coaching Agreement

B.
{ CO-CREATING THE RELATIONSHIP }

3. Establishing Trust and Intimacy with the Learner
4. Coaching Presence

C.
{ COMMUNICATING EFFECTIVELY }

5. Listening Actively
6. Questioning Powerfully
7. Communicating Directly

D.
{ FACILITATING LEARNING AND RESULTS }

8. Creating Awareness
9. Designing Actions
10. Planning and Goal Setting
11. Managing Progress and Accountability

For more information, visit www.coachfederation.org

L.E.A.D. Model

The L.E.A.D. model is a framework for a single coaching session. The questions on this and the subsequent page are suggestions, not a script. Don't expect to use all of the questions in any conversation. Let good listening, your own intuition and your learner's leadership challenge be your guide.

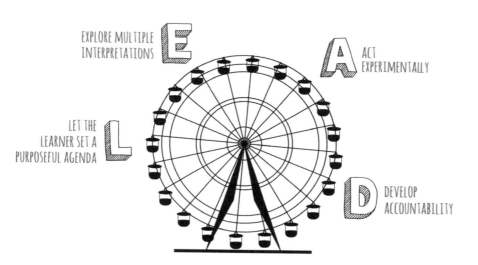

LET THE LEARNER SET A PURPOSEFUL AGENDA.

This is where the learner identifies a goal for the session and connects that goal to what really matters. In our brand of leadership coaching, the goal is in some way connected to a leadership challenge.

- What do you want to accomplish during this conversation?
- How might we know that we have accomplished it?
- How does this connect to your leadership challenge?
- If we're successful, what will you experience when we're done?
- What makes this session goal so important for you?
- What would real progress look like?
- How does this connect to your larger purpose (or values)?
- What leadership skills do you need to develop?

EXPLORE MULTIPLE INTERPRETATIONS.

This is the heart of the coaching session, where coach and learner partner to diagnose the situation from multiple points of view. The learner starts to generate options for experiments, most likely related to the four leadership competencies. (The Leadership Coaching questions of this book come in handy in this section.)

- What are adaptive and technical elements of the situation?
- Who else has a stake in the matter?
- What is their perspective? What would progress look like for them?
- What have you tried so far? What do you still need to explore or learn?
- What are other options? What else?
- What are the risks (related to each option)?
- What is your part of the mess?

ACT EXPERIMENTALLY.

This is the option-narrowing and reality-testing section of the coaching session. It's where the learner assesses the risks and chooses a course of action, which might include taking steps to further understand the situation.

- What experiment(s) will you try?
- How will you continue to learn, gain awareness or reflect on your situation?
- What do you think will happen as a result of each experiment?
- Whose support do you need?
- On a scale of 1 (low) to 10 (very high), how confident are you that you will actually do this? (If lower than 8, help the client rethink the experiment.)

DEVELOP ACCOUNTABILITY.

This is where coach and learner create a plan for action and support.

- What will you do and when will you do it?
- What do you hope to learn?
- How will we know that you've done it?
- How will you debrief and learn from each experiment?
- Whose support do you need as you move forward?

 COACHING TIP: *Spend 70 percent of the coaching session in the L. and E. sections of the model.*

Establishing the Coaching Relationship: Opening Session Guidelines and Questions

These are guidelines for your first session with a new learner. This is not a checklist. Do not expect to get through all of the material listed here. Listen actively and deeply to a learner, and follow the learner's lead. Use your intuition to choose where to go and what to ask.

1. Review and sign the coaching agreement.

(See sample on page 163.) Be sure to cover the following.

- Focus on leadership as described by the principles and competencies.

- Bias toward putting competencies into action (rather than talking about leadership).

- Confidentiality agreement.

- Duration of the agreement, meeting times and other logistics.

- If meeting online or by telephone, clarify whose responsibility it is to initiate the connection.

- Questions from the client about logistics, etc.

2. Describe your own approach to the coaching relationship.

- How you coach, or what the learner can expect of you.
- Benefits other learners have experienced through coaching with you.
- How the learner can make the most of coaching.

3. Ask about and discuss learner reservations and expectations.

- What reservations, if any, do you have about coaching?

- Do you have any particular concerns about working with me?

- Have you worked with a coach before? How did it go? (Discuss any unsatisfactory experience. Use it as information about the type of coaching that might work best for this learner.)

- What sense do you have about what would make this a really valuable relationship for you?

- What prompted you to choose me as your coach? This will help me better understand your expectations.

Set ground rules and commitments, such as the following:

- Conversations are confidential (with exceptions as stated in the coaching agreement).

- Both coach and learner commit to keeping appointments and beginning on time. (This is a good time to review your cancellation policy. Tell the learner how you will handle missed sessions without notice. Be specific about your expectations concerning advance time for rescheduling, and don't be afraid to treat your time just like you would any other valuable commodity.)

- Coach and learner agree to be direct and candid with each other, and to let one another know if something is not working or if needs are not being met.

5.

Set expectations about work between sessions, such as the following:

- Learner can expect to do work between sessions.
- Coach will hold learner accountable for agreements.

6.

Set expectations about preparing for sessions.

7.

Discover what's important to the learner by finding out about his or her self-perception and needs.

Ask questions such as the following:

- Who are you? Would you tell me about yourself and your organization?

- What would you like to know about me?

- I see in your application to this program that the issue that concerns you most is …

- Is there a story behind why that's so important for you?

- What would you like to be different in four months?

- How would you describe the gap between your current reality and your aspirations for yourself?

- What is your part of the mess? (How do you contribute to the gap?)

- What do you care enough about that you are willing to try something different?

8

If you are coaching in the midst of a leadership program, ask questions such as the following:

- What's this been like for you so far?
- What's most compelling?
- What's challenging?
- What have you noticed about yourself in this group?
- I know that you've begun to talk about the competency of "Manage Self." Have you had any insights related to that?
- Is there anything that you want to do differently when you rejoin the group?

9.

Help the learner think differently about leadership. Ask questions such as the following:

- What have you noticed about your own typical approach to leadership?
- How are you responding to the leadership competencies?
- What do you make of this idea that leadership is an action?
- What might you do differently? In the classroom? At home?

10.

Review commitments. Ask questions such as:

- What have we talked about that you want to remember?
- What perspective do you want to keep in mind?
- What has been most helpful?
- What can I do to be even more useful next time?

Coaching Agreement Example

This agreement is intended to outline the terms of the coaching partnership between _____ (Coach) and _____ (Learner), which is sponsored by (Sponsor).

This partnership, which has a limited time frame and focus on developing leadership capacity according to the KLC principles and competencies, is a process designed by the Coach and Learner.

Coaching, which is not advice, therapy, or counseling, may cover specific projects, leadership issues, life balance, career decisions, clarification of values and purpose, goal setting, accountability and any other business or personal issues the Learner wishes to address, within the context of leadership and making progress on adaptive challenges.

Confidentiality

The Coach promises that all the information shared by the Learner will be kept strictly confidential and will be shared with no one, including the Sponsor, without the Learner being present. The learner's willingness to disclose personal information and be truthful in order to accomplish objectives will be treated with utmost respect. This coaching relationship has a limited time frame, but this confidentiality agreement does not expire.

Professional development and program evaluation

The Coach requests the following exceptions to confidentiality for professional development and program evaluation purposes:

Permission to discuss a situation with his or her Mentor Coach for learning purposes;

Permission to share examples and experiences from coaching sessions –without using the Learner's name – with other Coaches and staff of the sponsor organization for learning and program development purposes;

Permission to report the Learner's name and number of coaching hours to the International Coach Federation for credentialing purposes; and

Permission to report the Learner's name and number of coaching hours to the sponsor for program evaluation purposes.

Communication

The power of the coaching relationship can be granted only by the Learner. Should the Learner feel that the coaching is not working as you wish, it is the Learner's responsibility to communicate with the Coach or Sponsor, so that action may be taken to return the power to the coaching relationship.

Agreement

Signatures indicate agreement with the terms outlined here.

_____   _____
Sponsor, date   Coach, date

_____
Learner, date

Leadership Coaching Questions

Powerful questioning is a core coaching competency identified by the ICF and practiced by coaches around the world to ensure effective communication. Leadership coaches ask questions that help learners better understand themselves and their situations while energizing others to work toward a shared purpose. The questions in this section are for you to use to help learners apply leadership competencies and principles to their real-world challenges.

These questions, which support attitudes and behaviors necessary to successfully exercise leadership on adaptive challenges, are grounded in our conviction that 21st-century organizations and communities need a profoundly different kind of leadership. They grow out of our belief that making progress on leadership challenges requires courageous collaboration from all levels and corners of a community, business or organization and engaging both usual and unusual voices to identify and solve problems. We encourage you to experiment with these questions as you coach. Use them to help your learners get comfortable with the language, concepts, attitudes and behaviors of effective leadership.

The first set of questions below is designed to help learners identify the adaptive and technical aspects of the challenges they face. Although leadership coaches are happy to help a learner outline the best approach to a technical problem, by far the greatest impact of our work is when we help foster the learning and motivation required to make progress on adaptive challenges. When you coach, the questions under Diagnose Situation will help you and learners generate insight into the technical and adaptive elements of a leadership challenge. Encourage learners to test assumptions and explore multiple interpretations. Use your questions to help learners attain a deeper level of understanding of the situations they face. Then call upon the questions under Manage Self, Intervene Skillfully and Energize Others to support learners in taking an active, experimental approach to leadership.

Like the questions in the L.E.A.D. Model, these are not meant to be a script. They are listed in no particular order, so use them in any combination you like. Listen actively, remain present and use your intuition. Weave these questions into the L.E.A.D Model. Change them.

Make them your own. Use questions to inspire learners to think in terms of progress, rather than quick fixes to their leadership dilemmas.

As you begin working with a new learner, and throughout the relationship, stay curious about what drives his/her desire to exercise leadership. Listen deeply for what really matters to learners, so that your questions arise out of the present moment and your authentic partnership. Ask questions such as:

- What issue or cause do you care deeply about?

- On behalf of what are you willing to do something differently?

- What makes you care so much?

- What values does your leadership challenge touch for you?

- What are you most concerned about?

- What are your aspirations?

Remember that coaching to make progress on adaptive challenges does not require knowing everything that is on a learner's heart or mind. Balance big-picture purpose questions that help a learner access intrinsic motivation to exercise leadership with questions that invite diagnosis of the environment in which the learner wants to make progress. More than that, be sure to balance diagnosis of self and situation with helping the learner remain accountable for taking action outside the coaching session, in the real world.

Each of the four leadership competencies has six dimensions. The coaching questions are grouped according to those competencies and bulleted descriptions.

Diagnose Situation

Questions related to this competency encourage learners to dig deeply beneath a given issue to uncover the history, conflicting loyalties, values and other complexities. Challenge yourself, when coaching around this competency, to ask questions that require a learner to make observations, look at the situation from multiple perspectives and test various interpretations of the situation. Rather than make suggestions, use open-ended questions that help learners draw on their own insights and experiences to design and choose interventions that are most likely to result in new learning about the people and context surrounding the challenge.

1.
Explore tough interpretations.

- Thinking about the adaptive elements of this issue, what's going wrong in the system?

- Who is the system working for?

- What needs to change?

- Who are the stakeholders? Who else? Who else? Anyone else?

- What work is being avoided? In what way?

- What if nothing changes?

- What aspirations do others have?

- How does the current reality contrast with your aspirations?

- What scares you?

- If you continue with business as usual, how much progress can you make?

2.
Distinguish technical and adaptive work.

- What could the right person fix right now?

- What technical fixes have you tried? How did that work?

- What feels really difficult?

- How do you know that this is an adaptive challenge?

- What values are at stake? What values does the group hold dear?

- What behaviors created the problem?

- What attitudes are typical of the group?

- What values, behaviors or attitudes might be in conflict with the work that needs to be done?

- How will you know when progress has been made?

- What is essential?

- Of your current practices, what will serve you in the future?

- What is expendable?

3.
Understand the process challenges.

- What makes leadership difficult on this issue?

- What processes have you tried?

- What's worked? What hasn't?

- How are people avoiding the problem?

- What alternative processes exist?

- If you had all the time in the world, how would you ease people into working together?

- What new process might you experiment with?

4.
Test multiple interpretations.

- If we'd just met, how would you describe the challenge?

- What other stories have you heard? Conflicting? Slightly differing?

- What do we know for sure?

- What is unknown?

- From your point of view, what needs to change?

- From the point of view of your biggest antagonist, what needs to change?

- Put yourself in the position of your grandchild or a great-niece or nephew, looking back at us from 50 years in the future. What story does he or she tell about how the problem was solved?

- Who needs to be engaged? Who else?

- What interpretations have you been unwilling to entertain?

- Thinking of unusual voices, who else should be at the table?

- What factions exist?

- What factions are you part of?

5.

Take the temperature.

- What's the temperature in the system? Too hot? Too cold?

- How do you know?

- Where is the conflict?

- Where is the pain or urgency?

- Who's working hard to maintain the current temperature? What's that about?

- What technical fixes have been tried? To what result?

- How are people feeling?

- How satisfied are you with the level of progress?

- Who is behaving badly? What problem are they trying to solve?

- What values are in conflict?

- How is that conflict showing up?

- Who has a stake in maintaining the status quo?

6.

Identify who needs to do the work.

- Whose problem is it? Who else?

- Who or what is pressuring you to take action?

- Who would be happy if you applied a quick technical fix?

- What story are various factions telling themselves about the adaptive challenge?

- What are they loyal to?

- What do they value?

- What do they stand to lose if change happens?

- What would success look like to each faction?

- What are you afraid to let go of?

- In your happiest dreams, who would step up and get involved?

Manage Self

Exercising leadership effectively requires the capacity to Manage Self. To foster learning and application of this competency, ask questions that help learners gain awareness of how others see them and what options are available. As you coach, use the following questions to challenge learner assumptions about strengths and weaknesses and to encourage them to experiment with a new repertoire of possible responses.

1.

Know your strengths, vulnerabilities and triggers.

- What are you really good at?
- How can you use those strengths?
- What are your weaknesses?
- How are they showing up in the situation?
- In what ways are you vulnerable?
- What gets your blood boiling?
- What values or needs (of your own) might be getting in your way?
- What's holding you back?
- What or who triggers you?
- What do you experience in your body (when you are triggered)?
- How will you manage that trigger?
- What would you like to learn?
- Who do you want to be?
- What is your role in this situation?
- Where is the rub between your "self" and your role?
- What are you avoiding?
- What would be different if you did not take things personally?
- What is the worst attack you could face?
- How will you prepare yourself for such an attack?
- Who or what benefits if you stay the same?
- What is threatened if you manage yourself?

2.
Know the story others tell about you.

- What are others saying about you? How do you know?

- What are your strengths in others' minds?

- Where are you in their story of this challenge?

- Describe your role from the point of view of a trusted colleague.

- Describe your role from the point of view of your biggest opponent.

- How are you part of the mess?

- What is your formal authority?

- What kind of informal authority do you have? With whom?

- How credible are you with each faction?

- How are you helping people avoid difficult work?

- How will you prepare yourself for such an attack?

- Who or what benefits if you stay the same?

- What is threatened if you manage yourself?

3.
Choose among competing values.

- What has held you back from intervening in the past?
- What risks have you been unwilling to take? Why?
- What would a big risk look like?
- What competing values are at play?
- What could you lose when you prioritize one value over another?
- What becomes possible if you choose one value over another?
- How will you prepare yourself for an attack?
- Who or what benefits if you stay the same?
- What is threatened if you manage yourself?

4.
Get used to uncertainty and conflict.

- What are you willing to put up with?
- What is impossible to tolerate?
- What are you risking?
- What will be difficult?
- What support do you need?
- Who will be disappointed?
- How will you keep from taking it personally?
- What makes it worth it?
- How will you know if you are becoming complacent?

5.

Experiment beyond your comfort zone.

- What unpopular action might lead to progress?

- What difficult choice could help?

- What would be the comfortable choice? What will you lose if you make it?

- What leadership styles or actions are uncomfortable for you?

- What uncomfortable choice, action or behavior might be useful in this situation?

- What holds you back from trying something different?

- Whose support will lessen the risk?

6.

Take care of yourself.

- On a scale of 1 (low) to 5 (high), what's your energy level right now?

- How you do engage in self-care?

- When are you most energized?

- What do you need to say no to?

- How will you take care of yourself right now?

- How will you stay connected to purpose?

- How do you know when your energy is waning?

- What (places, people, practices) revitalizes you?

- Who will support you?

176

Intervene Skillfully

Leadership starts with a personal intervention. Use these questions to help learners make skillful, conscious choices about whether, when and how to intervene. Pose questions that help a learner to gain insight that leads to action and progress.

1.
Make conscious choices.

- What type of leadership is necessary?
- What is the purpose of the intervention?
- Who shares that purpose?
- What does your gut tell you?
- What has already been tried?
- How did that go?
- What pushback can you expect?
- How will you handle it?
- What would you normally do?
- What could you try instead?
- What will success look like?
- How will you evaluate?

2.
Raise the heat.

- What work is being avoided?
- What conflict needs to be faced?
- What are the consequences of inaction?
- If you had no fear, what would you say?
- If you had no fear, what would you do?
- What do people need to wrestle with?
- What is the elephant in the room?
- What's the burning question you haven't asked?
- What's not being said?
- What are three ways you could raise the heat?

3.
Give the work back.

- If the work is adaptive, who are the stakeholders?
- What would it mean to give the work back?
- How can others help define the problem?
- Who has to be on board with the solution?
- Who needs to do what?
- What capacity does this group need to develop?
- How will you engage people (not just delegate)?

4.
Hold to purpose.

- What is your purpose?
- What distracts or diverts you?
- What re-orients you to purpose?
- How does that contribute to your purpose?
- How clear are others about your purpose?
- How can you make your purpose clearer?
- What's the big picture?
- What's negotiable? What's not?
- What are you willing to let go of?

5.
Speak from the heart.

- What makes this so important to you?
- What makes this so important to others?
- Why? Why? Why? Why? Why?
- What does your heart tell you when you listen to theirs?
- How will you share that with others?
- What story will you tell?
- What emotions will you name?
- What do you hope people learn?
- What do you want people to do?

6.
Act experimentally.

- What is the purpose of your experiment?
- What are you curious about?
- What do you want to have happen?
- What do you think will happen?
- What assumptions are you testing?
- What is the stretch for you?
- What is your plan?
- What is the time frame?
- On a scale of 1 (low) to 10 (high), where would you rate the risks?
- If you rated the risk at 6 or above, how can you take it down a point or two?
- How will you monitor progress?
- What did you learn?
- What will you try next?

Leadership on adaptive challenges requires energizing others. Use these questions to help learners engage more effectively by discovering connecting interests, attending to how people work together (the process) and inspiring them to keep at it, even when it's hard.

1.
Engage unusual voices.

- Who will be affected?
- Who has a stake but little influence?
- Who is not engaged?
- Who is at the table but not influencing the process?
- Who are the unusual voices in this situation?
- What do you need to do differently?
- What are you doing that is really someone else's work?
- How will you need to listen differently?
- What are the barriers?
- How will you meet them where they are?
- How will you create conditions for collaboration?
- What would a trustworthy process look like for them?

2.
Work across factions.

- What are the relevant factions?

- Who is against you?

- Who supports you?

- Who is neutral and necessary?

- Whom can you afford to ignore?

- For the faction you are focused on, what's their story about the adaptive challenge?

  – What are they loyal to?
  – What do they value?
  – What do they stand to lose if change happens?

- What would success look like to each faction?

- Whose help do you need?

  – Who influences that faction?

- How will you start?

- How will you listen?

- What questions do you need to ask?

- What is required of you?

- What bridges must you build?

- How slowly can you afford to go?

3.
Start where they are.

- What do they care about?

- What brought them here?

- What are they scared of? Intimidated by?

- What do they need?

- What gets them frustrated?

- What keeps them engaged?

- What's more important to them than your purpose?

- Where are they coming from? How do you know?

- How will you learn more?

- What's it like in their shoes?

- What do you lose if they help craft the vision?

- How will you engage them from the very beginning?

4.
Speak to loss.

- What is going to change?

- Who is going to lose what?

- What is the bad news?

- Who will be hit the hardest?

- How will you acknowledge the loss?
  – How will you name it?

- How will they know that you care?

- How hard will it be to listen through the pain?

- How will you manage yourself?

5.

Inspire a collective purpose.

- What is your purpose?

- What will progress look like?

- What small success can you achieve quickly?

- How will you celebrate?

- Who shares your purpose?

- Who else do you need to include?

- Who isn't inspired?

- What are your aspirations?

- Who shares that hope?

- Who needs to be brought along?

- What barriers exist?

6.
Build a trustworthy process.

- Who needs to trust you?

- What does trust mean in this situation?

- What are the barriers to trust?

- How flexible are you?

- How ready are people for change?

  – What would be too much change too quickly?
  – What would be too little?

- What process will you use to engage others?

- How can you encourage openness?

- How will you pace the work?

- Whose help do you need?

Concluding a Coaching Engagement: Final Session Guide

When you are wrapping up a coaching engagement, whether after three meetings or 30, help a learner articulate and appreciate the value and progress made through the coaching relationship. Try these questions to guide the conversation:

1. What is the most important thing you've learned through coaching?

2. What is the most important thing you've accomplished?

3. What is different about your leadership as a result of coaching?

4. What will you continue doing?

5. What will you change?

6. What unfinished business, if any, exists?

7. What story will you tell others about your coaching?

8. What will you miss about having a coach?

9. How will you build that into your life?

10. What (or whose) support do you need going forward?

If you've enjoyed the relationship, never hesitate to offer yourself as a resource for the future. Remind the learner that you are only a phone call away and welcome hearing about successes and talking through challenges. Leave the door open for another series of coaching conversations whenever the need arises to further develop capacity for leadership.

CHAPTER 4

Introducing the Principles and Competencies

Introducing the Principles and Competencies

Before you attempt new, provocative teaching methods such as Case-in-Point, it helps to feel confident that you can deliver the basics. For this reason, it made sense to us to include some specific things that you can do right away, sessions that allow you to introduce the KLC competencies to others without taking the risks inherent in Case-in-Point or case teaching. In this chapter, unlike the first three, the methods are familiar and the steps to success are clear.

1. Have a good outline.

2. Study the outline and learn to deliver key content.

3. Practice facilitating robust discussions in which everyone has a chance to participate. Find ways to engage the quiet people and hold back constant contributors.

4. Find a peer or mentor to observe you in action.

5. Invite your observer to answer these questions:
   - Did I deliver the content clearly? Did learners understand what I wanted them to know?
   - Did my facilitated discussions provide the foundation for all learners to engage experientially with the leadership principles and competencies?
   - What strengths did you see in my facilitating or teaching?
   - What do you recommend I do differently?

The teaching methods you read about in the first three chapters of this book — as well as the session outlines you are about to encounter

— are designed to help people learn skills to make lasting, positive change in their businesses, organizations and communities. They are based on the idea that leadership is an activity, not a particular role or position. Developing leadership capacity in others — the work you do — is adaptive work in that no expert can tell you exactly how to do it. You have to experiment. You have to diagnose your group and the needs of individuals within it. You have to start where they are by considering their values, loyalties and the potential losses associated with embracing a new approach to leadership. You need to manage yourself.

Realizing that leadership development is adaptive, we hesitated to provide session outlines. We feared that we would somehow give the impression that one size fits all. It doesn't. Yet, we know that it is helpful to see how others have approached a similar adaptive challenge. Put another way, why reinvent the wheel? Some things are technical challenges. In some areas, it makes sense to say, follow these steps if you want to achieve this set of learning outcomes. Therefore, in this chapter we offer examples of session outlines and leadership development activities that KLC teachers and coaches use to deliver content. Look them over, try them in the classroom, and get good at delivering them. Then, when you feel proficient, try using them as a jumping-off point for Case-in-Point, or as learning moments in the midst of case teaching, or to provide a new frame of reference for a coaching learner. When you try a new approach, please share what you discover with the authors of this book.

Diagnosing Your Situation

When it comes time for you to use the following outlines with a group, first take time to consider the diagnostic questions. Review them. Talk with others. Think deeply about the needs of your group before you start choosing topics and creating agendas. Extend your thinking to a diagnosis of yourself and your learning and development goals. Then use the relevant facts and insights, along with the material in this book to make choices and craft your agenda.

Diagnostic Questions

As you consider how to use and adapt the materials in this and other chapters, take time to analyze and understand the needs of your learners. Jot down responses to the following questions.

1. What is the purpose of the meeting or training session?

2. What do the people who hired/invited me expect?

3. How much time will I have with the group?

4. How many sessions will I have (one or more)?

5. What is the history of the group? Has it been together before? Is it an intact team? An ad hoc work group? What kinds of interpersonal dynamics are likely to be at play?

6. What does this group need to know? What do its members want to know?

7. What is the group's previous knowledge of the leadership principles and competencies?

8. What is the makeup of the group (age, authority level, etc.)?

9. What is the emotional state of the group? Is it facing a crisis? In a rut? Dissatisfied with the status quo?

10. What is at risk for members of the group? What are the issues they're facing?

11. How do members of this group talk with one another? What language do they use? (Use words that they will understand. Avoid jargon.)

12. Considering what I know about the group's situation, what particular concept would help? For instance:

- If I know the group is facing conflict, teach finding the productive zone of disequilibrium.
- If the group is going through a big transition, teach speaking to loss.
- If someone isn't at the table, teach engaging unusual voices.
- If the group needs to engage people who might not agree, teach working across factions.
- If the group seems to be rushing to solutions, teach distinguishing the difference between technical and adaptive work.

13. What specific challenges does this group face that may lead me to teach a specific competency?

14. Of all the leadership principles and competencies, what is likely to make the most difference for this group of learners?

15. What level of heat or discomfort can this group tolerate during a training session?

16. What will be the best delivery method(s) for this group?

Diagnose Yourself

Take time to consider your own personal, professional and financial development goals for the program.

1. What is most important for me to accomplish with this program? Is it to solidify a relationship with a learner? Market my services and talents? Push my edge as a trainer? Motivate a group that I am a member of? Some other goal?

2. How comfortable am I with the content I've chosen to deliver? Whose help do I need to get more comfortable?

3. What is my comfort level with the primary teaching methods described in Chapters 1–3? What teaching method(s) will I use in this program?

4. What are some risks I am willing to take to further my own development?

5. What would be too risky?

Once you have answered these diagnostic questions about yourself, you are ready to pinpoint your teaching goals and choose among potential methods and activities. To help you make your choices and achieve your goals, this chapter provides directions for sessions on a few key topics.

LIFE IN THE GAP: Leadership principles and competencies	**DIAGNOSE SITUATION:** Explore tough interpretations	**DIAGNOSE SITUATION:** The art of the debrief
DIAGNOSE SITUATION: Peer consultation	**MANAGE SELF:** Know your strengths, vulnerabilities and triggers	**MANAGE SELF:** Experiment beyond your comfort zone
ENERGIZE OTHERS: Faction mapping	**INTERVENE SKILLFULLY:** Raise the heat	**INTERVENE SKILLFULLY:** Act experimentally

Although this chapter does not cover everything it gives you what you need to introduce the principles and competencies and get learners started applying them in their work. These are the sessions we use most often in KLC programs, and we recommend them for you. You may choose to use them all in a brand-new leadership program or add one or two to your existing program.

Whether you are a rank beginner or have years of teaching or coaching under your belt, these descriptions provide

SHORTCUTS TO INTEGRATING THE KLC LEADERSHIP COMPETENCIES AND PRINCIPLES

in your work with adult learners.

Think of these as notes from your peers and as guidelines rather than scripts, or suggestions rather than strict instructions. Make them your own with anecdotes, examples and facilitation questions that fit your personality and the needs and character of your group.

Session 1

Life in the Gap: Leadership Principles and Competencies

Goals

The goals of this activity are to:

- Define the gap between the current situation and learner aspirations.

- Introduce the distinction between technical and adaptive work.

- Introduce the leadership principles and competencies as descriptors of the type of leadership it will take to make progress in the gap.

Materials

- Flip chart and markers.

Time

- 50–75 minutes.

Instructions

Facilitate this session in a large group, allowing learners to work individually or in small groups if necessary to engage everyone in the discussion.

Allow the group to consider the question, "When you think about the future of your group (company, organization, agency, community), what concerns you the most?" Write the question on a flip chart and list a couple of pages of responses. Help individuals to identify challenges they care about as concerns, not simply as issue areas; for instance, if education is listed as a concern, ask the participant, "So, more specifically, what concerns you about education?" Their response might be, "drop in graduation rates," "more and more children are not 'ready' for kindergarten," or "we see fewer students going on to post-secondary education." Or if you are working in a corporation and someone lists "our culture" as a concern, ask, "So, specifically, what concerns do you have about this culture?" Invite learners to summon the courage to name what bothers or upsets them as frankly as possible.

Put those concerns on your flip chart. Do not attempt consensus here. Simply get a short list of daunting concerns up on the wall.

Then, ask the group, "What are your aspirations?" Encourage them to explain what the world would look like if their concerns were addressed. List some aspirations on the flip chart.

When you have the two lists posted on the wall, stand in the middle. Raise the notion of a "gap" between aspirations and current situation.

Now ask, "What makes leadership difficult in the gap?" Focus learners on what makes leadership difficult for them personally, not for others such as authority figures. Again, the objective is to make these difficulties immediate and personal. You are likely to get answers such as, "polarization," "entrenched viewpoints," "the necessity to make a profit," "people in authority don't want to change how they operate," "complacency" and "apathy." You can also ask individuals to consider their own part of the mess. You may then begin to hear answers such as, "I get triggered when …," "I get overwhelmed when …," "I get caught up in my little world when …," etc.

Introduce the idea that one of the things that makes leadership on these challenges so difficult is that this is adaptive work.

Tell the group, "An adaptive challenge consists of a gap between the aspiration and current reality that demands responses outside the repertoire — you don't have the information you need or a protocol you can follow." Addressing an adaptive challenge requires moving people from the status quo by engaging and challenging both their hearts and their minds.

199

TECHNICAL PROBLEMS

are easy to recognize, and you either know how to solve them or can access the experience to make progress.

Adaptive challenges are different; they are not clearly defined and require learning to understand what is going on. The solutions also require learning to develop new tools, methodologies and practices.

For example, you go to the doctor with a broken arm. The problem is complex, but there is a clear solution, and you can access hundreds of doctors who can fix the problem. What if you have high cholesterol? That is a different kind of problem. Your doctor can prescribe medication, but she can't change the way you eat or make you exercise. This is an adaptive challenge: the work belongs to you, your family and even your co-workers. You will have to give up something you love, perhaps ice cream after dinner with the kids, or an extra hour in bed so you can get to the gym.

ADAPTIVE CHALLENGES

are about changing priorities, beliefs, habits and loyalties for a compelling purpose.

Introduce the idea that most problems have both technical and adaptive elements. Draw the chart in Figure 20 to outline key distinctions between technical and adaptive work.

Distinguishing Technical and Adaptive Work

DISTINGUISHING TECHNICAL AND ADAPTIVE

	TECHNICAL WORK	ADAPTIVE WORK
THE SOLUTION	...is clear	... requires learning
THE PROBLEM	... is clear	requires learning
WHOSE WORK IS IT?	experts or authority	stakeholders
TYPE OF WORK	efficient	act experimentally
TIMELINE	ASAP	longer term
EXPECTATIONS	fix the problem	make progress
ATTITUDE	confidence and skill	curiosity

Now ask the group, "What type of leadership will it take to make progress on the deep, daunting, adaptive challenges facing our company, organization or community?" Listen and then point out the leadership principles and competencies (on the wall or in their copy of "For the Common Good: Participant Handbook").

Conclude with an overview of central points from this session to set the stage for the rest of the program.

- Not enough progress is being made on adaptive challenges. The "gap" remains in spite of our best efforts.

- Challenges require adaptive as well as technical work.

- Current leadership practices are inadequate.

- We need more purposeful, provocative and engaging leadership practices such as those in the KLC framework.

Delivery Tips

This is a low- to medium-heat facilitated session, but opportunities for some Case-in-Point work may arise. To accommodate different learning and engagement styles, move back and forth from personal reflection time, paired or small-group exchanges and large-group discussion. It is useful to record some of the ideas from each step on flip charts for teaching purposes and future reference, if this can be done in an efficient, non distracting way. Work with a partner if you can to make the note-taking less intrusive. The recording doesn't need to be exhaustive. Try to recognize when enough is enough to get the point across and move on. It's easy to get bogged down and lose track of time and have to force the concluding points.

This session works best in a longer program when establishing a rationale or foundation for KLC's ideas helps support subsequent work. You may choose not to use it in favor of other activities in a short-form program if your objective is to help learners immediately apply one or more competencies or principles in their own work.

Links to For the Common Good: Participant Handbook

- Chapters 1, 3 and 4 are useful pre-reading for participants in this session.

Session 2

Diagnose Situation:
Explore Tough Interpretations

Goals

This session asks learners to move beyond interpretations that are technical, benign and individual in nature. It prepares them to exercise leadership imagining and explore interpretations that are more adaptive, conflictual and systemic. In it, you teach and support participants in learning to:

- Distinguish between observations and interpretations.

- Understand the difference between benign and conflictual, technical and adaptive, and individual and systemic interpretations.

- Practice generating, testing and holding multiple interpretations that are more adaptive, conflictual and systemic.

Materials

- Flip chart and markers, or laptop and slide projector.

Time

- 30–60 minutes

Instructions

Set the stage by introducing the competency of Diagnose Situation. Make the points that:

- Groups often generate action steps before spending adequate time diagnosing the situation; and

- To build a new muscle, we are going to stay in a diagnostic mode for longer than most of us are used to or comfortable with.

Then, teach the distinction between observations and interpretations (write these on a flip chart).

OBSERVATION:

A detailed examination of phenomena prior to interpretation. Observing is the act of noticing, with your senses, the details, events and patterns around you (or in your own body).

INTERPRETATION:

Explanation of the meaning of observations. Interpreting assigns meaning to acts.

Ask learners to practice being clear about whether they are making observations or interpretations. Tell them you will be encouraging them to push beyond a first interpretation to generate multiple interpretations.

Raise the question, "Why focus on interpretations? Why might generating multiple interpretations be an act of leadership?"

Facilitate their answers or share your own: "Exercising leadership requires both being involved in the daily action and rising above to view the broader dynamics and patterns surrounding you. We sometimes call this moving from the dance floor to the balcony. A significant challenge, when we look down from the balcony, is to see the data for what it is, rather than censoring the data you don't want to see. Too often we pay attention to some dynamics and ignore others."

Turn the group's attention to something that has been discussed in the room since you have been together. You may choose an interaction from a case study, or something from a learner's leadership challenges. Or it may be an exchange between two group members or between a learner and the teacher. Ask members of the group to describe what they *observed* about the event.

If the group is mixing observations with interpretations (groups usually make that mistake at first), help them understand the difference. Ask the group, "What did you observe?" Explain that "observe" means, "What did you see? What did you hear? What did you directly experience?"

After learners have voiced several observations, ask them to move on to interpretations. In other words, ask people to explain the potential meaning behind what they observed.

At some point after someone has made an interpretation, ask the same person to provide another interpretation. Explain that "your first interpretation is your opinion, and we are interested in hearing another interpretation that may or may not be an opinion you hold." Push several people to make more than one interpretation.

When learners have caught on to the concept of multiple interpretations, you can begin to help them move beyond the easy ones. Initial interpretations are often technical, benign and individual, but

CONSIDERING TOUGH INTERPRETATIONS IS A LEADERSHIP BEHAVIOR.

Ask learners to take the risk of sharing interpretations that are more adaptive, conflictual and systemic. By systemic, we mean having to do with the dynamics of the group, its context or the culture in which the group operates.

Introduce the interpretation chart. Draw it on a flip chart.

FIGURE 21:

Interpretation Chart

MULTIPLE INTERPRETATIONS

TECHNICAL ➤ ADAPTIVE

BENIGN ➤ CONFLICTUAL

INDIVIDUAL ➤ SYSTEMIC

Tell the group that the table in Figure 21 shows the shift in interpretations that people exercising leadership must grapple with to make progress on adaptive challenges.

Say something like, "Your goal is to move from the default interpretations, which tend to be technical, benign and individually focused. Nudge yourself and others toward interpretations that are adaptive, conflictual and systemic."

Facilitate discussion on the consequences of this interpretive shift. Ask learners:

- What would happen if you diagnosed your situations with more adaptive conflictual and systemic interpretations?

- What would change in this room if we started diagnosing our situation with more adaptive, conflictual and systemic interpretations?

If you are using the "For the Common Good: Participant Handbook," point learners to the Testing Interpretations section. Give them time to reflect in writing, noting the Testing Interpretations section that they and others are using to explain aspects of their issue. This activity works well after faction mapping has been introduced.

Links to Participant Handbook

This session links directly to Testing Interpretations.

Session 3

Diagnose Situation: The Art of the Debrief
Goals

A debrief is a short timeout from the action of Case-in-Point, a case study or other experiential learning session.

The purpose is disciplined reflection, an opportunity for learners to solidify lessons about leadership and
CONSIDER HOW THEY WILL APPLY THEM TO CHALLENGES IN THE OUTSIDE WORLD.

Your job is to invite participants up to the balcony and help them identify more options for leadership than were apparent in the midst of the action. Formal debriefs help deepen understanding and encourage application of key concepts. The debrief is not a time to recap learning, restate key ideas or introduce new content.

Take care not to let the debrief become a replay of conversations that have already taken place. Ask provocative questions and leave plenty of space for participants to make meaning of their own.

Like the rest of your program or session, each debrief should challenge learners to think differently and practice new behaviors.

Time

- 20–45 minutes

Instructions

1. Take a few minutes to orient the group to the idea of debriefing a classroom session. Share the purpose of a debrief. Consider explaining what makes a good debrief and signs that the debrief might be on the wrong track.

2. Ask a simple open-ended question (see examples below). Get learners talking as quickly as possible. This is not the time to share your own thoughts. Instead, create space for the group members to express themselves.

3. Identify a time frame for the debrief and stick to it. There may be temptation to extend beyond the time boundary, especially if the debrief is revealing intriguing ideas and interpretations about your group. Stick with your schedule. This is not the time to solve issues related to your group, but rather to engage in a different style of learning.

Examples of Debrief Questions:

- **What is on your mind?**

- **What thoughts, reflections, or observations do you have?**

- **How would you describe the way this group works together?**

- **How have we modeled (or not) the leadership ideas we are exploring?**

- **What are our adaptive challenges as a group?**

- **What is going on for you in this program?**

- **What hidden issues may be affecting learning?**

- **What assumptions are being challenged?**

- **How does what's happening here reflect processes at work or in your community?**

- **What word or words describe where you are with this process?**

- **How might we interpret these words?**

- **What concerns you the most about bringing these ideas back to your organization/community?**

Elements of a Good Debrief:

- It is provocative; the group explores the "song beneath the words," examining the learner experience so far.

- Teachers and learners make interpretations that are adaptive, systemic and tough.

- Learners share conflicting perspectives.

- It covers new ground, including insights into the dynamics at play in the room.

- Learners gain insight into how the system is functioning (i.e., the factions in the room, who feels they are risking something, how individuals are responding to each other, what learning is taking place, etc.).

- It is an opportunity for the teachers to test their interpretations about how the group is operating.

Signs a Debrief may be on the Wrong Track

- The conversation during the debrief sounds just like the one you are supposed to be debriefing (for instance, the same people are doing most of the talking).

- The energy and heat in the room are low.

- Reflections and discussion are about the content rather than the process (the way the group has been working together).

Session 4

Diagnose Situation: Peer Consultation
Goals

The goal of this session is to give learners multiple opportunities to practice diagnostic skills. The session speeds understanding of adaptive work by engaging learners in dialogue about their own adaptive challenges in a small group setting.

Learners will:

- Ask provocative questions, bring hidden issues to the surface and offer insights about leadership challenges; and

- Engage with peers in diagnosing situations, testing multiple interpretations and designing skillful interventions to make progress on their leadership challenges.

The process has been successful if learners:

1. Articulate and act on the distinction between diagnosis and action;

2. Articulate new perspectives on and insights into their own and others' leadership challenges;

3. Begin to ask more provocative questions and make tough interpretations about their own and others' leadership challenges; and

4. Begin to experiment with interventions outside their comfort zones within the group.

Peer consultation is a structured exercise confined to specific time frames. It starts with a demonstration of the process in the large group, then learners move to small groups in which each person has the opportunity to present a challenge for consultation by peers. For the large-group demonstration, choose someone in advance who has submitted a leadership challenge that is truly adaptive in nature. Talk with that individual ahead of time to make sure he or she is comfortable talking about that challenge in front of everyone and willing to listen to tough questions and feedback in a large-group setting.

The goal of the exercise is to focus the group on developing diagnostic skills, those that will help participants uncover the systemic dimensions of their leadership challenges (i.e., thinking about interpretations that are adaptive, conflictual and systemic). It is designed to create opportunities for participants to practice working on adaptive challenges with peers.

Materials and Room Setup

See the Peer Consultation section of the "For the Common Good: Participant Handbook." You will need:

- Five or six chairs in a semicircle at the front of the room;

- A separate room or table for each Peer Consultation group; and

- Slides of the process, projector and screen (optional).

Time

- 70 minutes for the demonstration.

- 50 minutes for each person in a small group to present and get consultation, or approximately five hours for a group of five learners.

Instructions

You will need a volunteer case presenter plus four or five peer consultants for the demonstration. For demonstration purposes, it works best when the peer consultants have experience with the process and can skillfully deliver provocative questions and tough, adaptive and systemic interpretations.

Direct participants to the Peer Consultation section of the "For the Common Good: Participant Handbook" and ask them to follow along as you give instructions. Call their attention to the Traps to Watch Out For section.

Start your demonstration by going swiftly over those pages with the group, perhaps with the aid of a projector and slides. From the start of your demonstration, reinforce the importance of strictly following the instructions for roles, process and time. Tell your group that this process was developed by Cambridge Leadership Associates and fine-tuned by KLC. It has been used with corporate, military and community groups around the world. Experience shows that learners get the most value when they follow the process exactly.

For the purposes of the demonstration, take a two- or three-minute break between each section of the peer consultation process (outlined in Figure 22) to answer questions.

Peer Consultation Process

Case presentation **5 minutes**	**Goal for Case Presenter:** To present a leadership challenge • What is the adaptive challenge? • Who are the major players? What are their conflicting perspectives and interests? • What are your strengths with the major players? • What action have you taken or are thinking about taking in reference to the challenge? • What are your real stakes and interests? • Are there any hidden issues? • What have I learned about my adaptive challenge so far?
Data gathering questions **10 minutes**	**Goal for group:** To understand the adaptive challenge and the complexities surrounding it and to gather information to help you conduct diagnostic brainstorming in the next phase. • Who are the major players? What are their formal relationships? Informal alliances? • Where is the senior authority on the issue? • Who are the unusual voices in this situation, and have you sought them out? • What has the presenter done so far to work on the problem? What has the presenter decided not to do? • Why are you working on this? • What do you care about related to this challenge? • What would success look like to the presenter?
Diagnostic brainstorming **15 minutes** **NOTE: Case Presenter does not speak.**	**Goal for group:** To interpret what is happening, offer alternative interpretations and illuminate new ways to understand the case. • What are the case presenter's stakes: risk of real or anticipated loss, sense of personal competence, pressure to maintain loyalties? • What issues or values does the presenter represent in the case? Do you see/hear competing values? • What are the underlying or hidden issues? What are the value choices each has to make? • How does the situation look to the other players? What is the story they are telling themselves? • What options are off the table for the presenter and why? • What has the presenter contributed to the problem? What is her/his piece of the mess? • What possible adaptive, conflictual or systemic interpretations has the presenter been understandably unwilling to consider? • What is the level of disequilibrium in the system? • What are the relevant factions in this challenge, and what do they care about, who are they loyal to and what are some of their potential losses? • For real change to happen, who has to do the work on this? Who else? • What would it look like for the presenter to "start where they are"? • What would success look like to the players other than the presenter?

Action Step Brainstorming
5 minutes
NOTE: Case Presenter does not speak.
	Goal for Group: To offer possible new initiatives, smart risks and experiments for the case presenter to try to move the challenge forward.
	• What smart experiments could be undertaken? Which KLC leadership competency subpoints seem relevant?
	  – Does the presenter need to raise or lower the heat?
	  – How might the presenter need to "manage self" differently?
	  – What would it look like for the presenter to "start where they are"?
	• What are low-risk tests of some of the ideas discussed?
	• What courageous conversations need to take place?
	• What new partnerships or relationship shifts need to happen?
	• What could the presenter watch for or monitor as signs of progress on this adaptive challenge?

Presenter reflections **5 minutes**	Goal for Case Presenter: Not to resolve the case. This time is intended for the presenter to share initial reactions to the process and ask specific questions that he/she is now pondering. • Comment on what has been heard. The idea is that the presenter will "rent" the ideas, trying them out rather than "buying" them or defending against them. • Identify any action step(s) you might undertake in the next six weeks.
Group debrief **5 minutes**	**Goal for group:** To "get on the balcony" and reflect on how well the consultation went and how to improve in the future. • What did the group accomplish and what did it avoid? • What default behaviors did participants observe? • Did we make adaptive, conflictual and systemic interpretations? • Did we identify the adaptive challenge? • What could be done to improve consultations in the future?

Session 5

Manage Self: Know your Strengths, Vulnerabilities and Triggers

Goals

Help learners manage themselves by identifying strengths, vulnerabilities and triggers that affect their ability to lead.

Materials

- The Diagnose Yourself Faction Map in the "For the Common Good: Participant Handbook."

- Flip chart and markers.

Time

- 30–45 minutes.

Instructions

Begin with a short presentation defining strengths, vulnerabilities and triggers and making the case that knowing oneself and how one is likely to react can improve chances of leading successfully and making progress on adaptive challenges. You might say:

"A big part of exercising leadership is understanding and appreciating our humanness, which can be summed up in our strengths, vulnerabilities and triggers. … If you are unable to manage yourself, trying to mobilize others will not just be incredibly frustrating, but we could argue that it could be impossible. By knowing your strengths, vulnerabilities and triggers, you will not only have a better chance of having them under control, but also at being intentional about how they can help you, or get in the way, when you exercise leadership."

Post the following definitions on a flip chart.

Strengths: Those aspects of the leadership competencies that come most naturally to you. (Explain that knowing which behaviors come easily will help us each choose the experiments and interventions most likely to lead to success.)

Vulnerabilities: Weak points of any sort — personal, organizational or historical; anything about your personality, position, skills or background that could derail your attempts at leadership. (If you have time, explain that vulnerability comes from a Latin word that means "a wound." Our human nature is to hide these wounds, oftentimes even from ourselves. We expend energy trying to conceal vulnerabilities and, when they are uncovered, to mitigate or minimize them. A wiser path may be to lean into vulnerabilities. Coolly acknowledging them, if only to yourself, can lead to better decisions and better leadership.)

Triggers: Any action, behavior, event or idea that simply sets you off — negatively or positively — and ends with you reacting more out of emotion than out of logic and strategy. (If time permits, use the following example and explanation: A trigger might be a certain individual speaking up in a staff meeting, a comment your spouse says from time to time or the fact that you were or weren't invited to a certain meeting. We all have them. And it's hard to lead if we can't manage them. Mindfulness is needed to control our triggers and how we respond. We must create a buffer zone between the trigger/impulse and our reaction. It is difficult to do adaptive work, to learn, to be open to new ideas, to explore multiple ways forward when we are acting out of emotion. Inability to control your triggers is a surefire way to fail in exercising leadership.)

Facilitate a short discussion of these definitions, making sure group members understand them sufficiently to embark on the self-reflection that follows. Then ask an opening question that gets people interacting and thinking about how they could be doing a better job of self-management, or request a show of hands in response to a couple of statements, such as:

- Raise your hand if you've ever let one of your own triggers get in the way of making progress on something you care about.

- Raise your hand if you've ever attempted to lead, and realized only after the fact that you failed to truly leverage your own strengths.

Then, tell the group that to lead effectively in corporate or community life, you need to know and manage yourself. You can make more progress on an issue if you are aware of your default reactions, if you know who and what is likely to trigger you.

Introduce the idea that you are going to give participants time to think about managing themselves as it relates to an issue they care about. Ask them to work individually to think about the different groups or factions they need to engage to make progress on their issue. Prepare them to challenge their own assumptions about strengths and vulnerabilities with each group. Encourage them to go a step further and consider how others see them, what stories other people are telling about their effectiveness. Underline the idea that the more we know and understand about our own strengths, vulnerabilities and triggers, the greater our repertoire of possible responses.

Refer learners to the Diagnose Yourself Faction Map in the "For the Common Good: Participant Handbook."

Direct learners to write their issue in the center of the diagram. Continue your directions with words such as, "Use the center section to reflect on how you perceive your role in the situation. Then jot down the names of key factions, considering your strengths and vulnerabilities with each. Think carefully about the story each faction is telling about you and your leadership."

If you have extra time, have learners share their diagrams with a partner. Ask them to consider possible things they might try to learn more about the strengths and vulnerabilities of each faction. Conclude the session by asking a few learners to talk about the value of taking time to assess your own strengths, vulnerabilities and triggers in relation to a specific leadership challenge.

Session 6

Manage Self: Experiment Beyond Your Comfort Zone

Goal

Teach the leadership behavior of experimentation beyond individual comfort zones, one aspect of the competency Manage Self. Learning objectives are to:

- Reinforce the concept that leadership begins with a personal intervention.

- Use the personal bandwidth diagram to teach people the value of stretching beyond their default behaviors and to experiment with new ways of deploying themselves as they exercise leadership.

Materials

- Flip chart and markers.

Time

- 10–75 minutes (see options, below).

Instructions

Introduce the idea that to be more effective in your leadership, it is worth pausing to determine how best to deploy yourself. That includes understanding your strengths and getting curious about where you might need to develop skills or call up some courage.

Introduce the Beyond Your Comfort Zone diagram.

FIGURE 23:

Beyond Your Comfort Zone

- **Q:** What makes it worth it?

- **A:** Your commitment to a purpose strong enough to compel you to do something different.

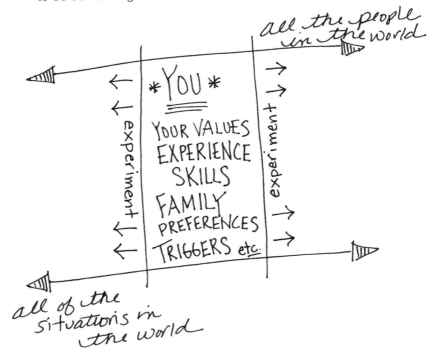

Tell the group, "The top horizontal line represents all the world's people. The bottom line represents all the world's situations. The space between the two parallel solid lines in the middle is you, everything about you, such as how you are packaged, your background and training, the lessons and hard wiring laid down by your parents, your upbringing, the advice and guidance you have received from mentors and friends, what you have learned from the school of hard knocks and the way you typically behave as a result."

"WE REFER TO THE WAY WE TYPICALLY BEHAVE AS OUR DEFAULTS."

The space between the two parallel lines in the middle of the situation horizontal is the range of situations in which you are especially well suited to intervene. This diagram suggests two leadership realities.

1. To be effective, you need to understand yourself pretty well, who you are and who you are not, your skills and your vulnerabilities, and the way others see and/or experience you (especially if that is different from the way you see and/or experience yourself). And you have to be able to be realistic in diagnosing the situation you are stepping into.

2. Look at the arrows. If you could expand your repertoire beyond the solid vertical lines in either direction, suddenly there would be a whole new set of situations in which you were well situated to intervene.

At this point, you can make a decision to move to Case-in-Point or facilitate a conversation using the following questions.

- What keeps us between these lines?

- What are the external forces in this room that are keeping you between the lines?

- What are the threats to the system we are in if you were to expand?

- Have you witnessed others managing their default behavior and/or changing their approach to enable their own or others' learning?

- What have you been willing to do to promote learning in this group?

- What are you unwilling to do?

- What opportunity exists in this system/room for you to stretch beyond your comfort zone?

- What would it look like for you to exercise leadership within this group?

- What roles have you seen played in this room?

- How do you think others have perceived your role in this system?

Conclude with an overview of the main points from this session.

- Exercising leadership begins with a personal intervention.

- We can increase our leadership effectiveness by understanding ourselves well.

- Expanding our personal bandwidth will increase our leadership capabilities.

- If we stay in our wheelhouse, if we do not change, we can't expect our communities to change.

- Getting beyond the status quo requires us to do something different from what the world expects us to do based on past performance.

Remind the group, "We will only take the risk of trying something new if we deeply care about the outcome or situation. We must be motivated by purpose."

Links to Participant Handbook

Leverage Your Strengths and Address Your Vulnerabilities.

Experiment Beyond Your Comfort Zone.

Options

You might simply introduce the visual and teach the value of experimenting outside your comfort zone. From there, you can use that aspect of Manage Self in your discussion of a leadership case study or move the group (or an individual you are coaching) directly to the participant handbook. Likewise, you might pause in the midst of a Case-in-Point session to draw the visual and encourage people to move outside the zone right here and right now. (Experiential learning at its finest!)

Session 7

Energize Others: Faction Mapping

Goals

The purpose of this session is to build the capacity of learners to visualize the competing values and conflicting priorities at work in any system with multiple factions. During the session, learners will:

1. Understand that making progress on any adaptive challenge requires engagement of diverse stakeholder groups, also known as factions, each holding unique points of view based on values, loyalties and perceived risks and potential losses.

2. Diagnose competing values through faction mapping.

3. Become aware that they each represent factions and contribute to the lack of progress on an issue they care deeply about.

Materials

- Flip chart and markers

Time

- 45–75 minutes.

Instructions

Start by identifying an adaptive challenge that is alive in the room among the learners; avoid lack of "issue" clarity, because it will hamper identification of factions with a stake in making progress on the challenge. In many situations, KLC faculty use "learning about leadership" as the adaptive challenge that is real for everyone in the classroom.

Using the Faction Map in the Participant Handbook as your guide, draw a map on the flip chart. Write your challenge in the center and ask the group to begin to identify relevant factions (that may either contribute to or impede progress on the challenge).

For example, "learning about leadership as a group" is a challenge with adaptive components that require stakeholder involvement: factions include those who value "content" over "process" and vice versa and those who feel like outsiders versus those who are well acquainted with KLC, etc. Although these examples are dichotomous, not all factions require paired opposites. The adaptive challenge of downtown redevelopment has many factions that are not necessarily in direct opposition to another identified faction. Push the group to identify a number of factions to avoid linking one faction to just one other faction. This will also make for more possibilities when brainstorming ways to work across factions.

As you create the Faction Map, encourage individuals to include themselves in one or more factions. An important part of the process is to see themselves as "part of the mess."

When the group has named seven to 10 factions, choose two or three and challenge the full group to identify the following.

- Values and deeply held beliefs, often which are based in a significant life experience and/or how you were raised.

- Loyalties, which are best defined as dedication to a group, a place or a way of doing things. This aspect of faction mapping is often overlooked; however, many groups have commented that loyalties actually trump values when guiding behavior in the community/ organizational arena. Law enforcement or political party members are often under tremendous pressure to "dance with the one who brung them" rather than cross factions or begin to better understand another faction's viewpoint.

- Losses/risks, as stakeholders, we do not necessarily fear change as much as we fear loss. We anticipate loss and see this as a risk we may not be willing to take. This may be loss of control, loss of prestige, loss of comfort or loss of familiarity.

Break people into small groups and ask each group to name values, loyalties and losses for two additional factions. Press the group to have a deep experience with faction mapping by brainstorming multiple interpretations of what a faction might value or fear losing. The deeper the diagnosis, the better chance individuals and groups will find commonalities to bridge factions as they go forward. It is interesting (and helpful to learning) to allow a group to identify factions without a lot of guidance from the teacher. This will help them gain confidence in their ability to diagnose.

Using the "vegetable stew" metaphor can be helpful when making the point that stakeholders are often represented by individuals or small representative groups (specific vegetables) who must return to their faction and explain why they have been changed by the collaborative process (why they now smell like other vegetables). This story also helps learners understand that unless the heat is raised on an issue (and the vegetables actually "stew"), very little shared understanding, compromise or collaboration will take place. One process consideration: This story may be distracting if it is used primarily to meet the group's need to be entertained by the teacher and the teacher's need to be entertaining.

FIGURE 24:

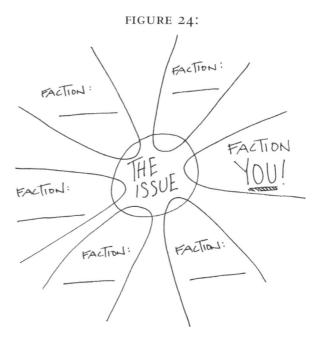

FACTION:

FACTION:

FACTION

FACTION:

THE ISSUE

YOU!

FACTION:

FACTION:

Links to the Participant Handbook

The Faction Map prompts learners to determine the degree to which each faction is needed to make progress. This allows you to point out that not all factions are equal. Some may be needed more than others to make progress on the identified issue. This will help learners to create strategies to engage critical stakeholders and might be used to introduce the idea of accepting (in some cases) that some stakeholders will not engage and can be accepted as "casualties."

The participant handbook includes a kind of "reverse faction map" titled Diagnose Yourself. This is important to note for two reasons. First, it is not a faction map and should not be confused with the one titled Faction Map. Second, it is an additional reason why faction mapping is helpful. The factions identified through Diagnose Yourself should be represented on (transferred to) the Faction Map. Looking at ourselves through the lenses of other stakeholders is a critical competency ("know the story others tell about you").

Session 8

Intervene Skillfully: Raise the Heat
Goals

The purpose of this session is to explore the idea that making progress on issues that we care about requires us to raise the heat on ourselves and others to do difficult work.

By the end of this session, learners will:

- Define "heat" as productivity in all its forms.

- Explore distinctions between heat, conflict and competing values.

- Discuss possible reasons for creating, exposing or elevating heat.

- Discuss the idea that raising the heat is necessary to progress.

- Understand the Productive Zone of Disequilibrium and its relationship to heat in the system.

Learners may also begin to:

- Assess the heat in the room.

- Explore their own comfort/discomfort with raising heat.

- Assess the heat around an issue they care about.

- Discuss when to elevate the heat.

- Examine the possible consequences and risks of raising the heat.

- Begin to practice methods for raising the heat.

Materials

- Flip chart and markers

- The Productive Zone visual

Time

- 30–75 minutes.

Instructions

Introduce the Productive Zone of Disequilibrium using this chart. The concepts in this graph come to us from our friends at Cambridge Leadership Associates.

FIGURE 25:

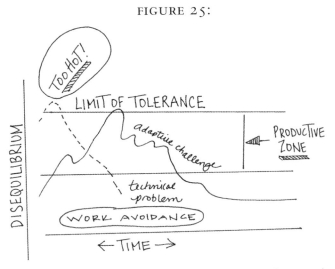

Tell the group, "To address adaptive challenges, you have to help people navigate through a period of disturbance as they sift through what is essential and what is expendable, and as they experiment with solutions to the adaptive challenges at hand. This disequilibrium can catalyze everything from conflict, frustration and panic to confusion, disorientation and fear of losing something dear. Adaptation occurs when there is some disequilibrium to the status quo. Without enough disequilibrium, nothing happens. But if there is too much disequilibrium, the situation gets too hot and we are driven by fight, flight or freeze responses. Above a threshold of change and below a limit of tolerance, lies a productive zone of disequilibrium."

229

Have learners reflect individually and identify examples (meetings, discussions or events they have been involved in, read about or seen in movies) when the disequilibrium went up and when it went down.

Sharing in groups of two or three, ask learners to explore the following questions:

- What caused the change in disequilibrium?

- What was the consequence on the group's work?

- What examples can you think of where a group stayed in the productive zone long enough to make progress?

Discuss in the large group. Ask:

- In what ways have you seen people successfully intervene to raise the heat when a group was below the productive zone? Make a list on the flip chart.

- When have you seen people intervene to lower the heat? Was the intervention productive?

- What interventions have raised or lowered the heat in this room?

If learners do not bring up the following, you may wish to interject them into the discussion.

Interventions that could raise the heat:

- Ask people "why" rather than letting their assertions/statements stand.

- Make provocative interpretations (systemic, conflictual, adaptive).

- Impose deadlines.

- Make a compelling case about what is not working in the current system.

- Create groups of people that combine the usual and the unusual voices.

- Shine light on the elephants in the room and address rumors.

Interventions that could lower the heat:

- Take a break.

- Tell a joke.

- Take the conversation out of the room.

If there is time, ask learners to reflect individually and share in pairs about their own limit of tolerance. Ask them to consider:

- When was the last time you had a fight, flight or freeze response?

- What triggered you into that reaction?

- What was lost when you reached that limit of tolerance?

- What might you have done to stay engaged?

Links to Participant Handbook

The Take the Temperature section can be used several times throughout the session, such as when asking learners about the temperature in the room throughout the session, about the temperature at any given moment, and about the temperature related to the issue they are working through at work or in their community.

The Raise the Heat section prepares the way for discussion of raising the heat and helps learners think about how they could intervene more successfully to make progress on their challenges.

Sharing the adaptive work with everyone who has a stake in the challenge is a strategy for raising heat. The Give the Work Back section allows learners to explore what they have done and what else they might do to give work back.

Options

1. Combine this activity with a case study. Every leadership case prepared by KLC provides an opportunity to question learners about levels of shared productivity, sources of the heat, observations about who is experimenting with raising the heat, the learning being generated, and the consequences of raising the heat.

2. After learners identify their individual leadership challenges using the Leadership Challenge section in the participant handbook, they can diagnose the heat surrounding their issue and design experiments around raising the heat and moving the issue/factions into a productive zone of work.

Session 9

Intervene Skillfully: Act Experimentally
Goals

This session is designed to give learners the opportunity to think about and develop, in writing, some possible smart experiments for making progress on their particular leadership challenge. Once the possible experiments are recorded, participants can assess the actual potential of trying the experiment and consider the potential outcome.

This exercise relates to the following competencies and subpoints: Manage Self (experiment beyond your comfort zone; get used to uncertainty and conflict) and Intervene Skillfully (make conscious choices; act experimentally).

Objectives of this session are to:

- Teach or reinforce the idea of smart risks. Tell people to think about trying to change only 5 percent of their behavior. Acknowledge that learners have many gifts, talents and capabilities but should think about what 5 percent of their behavior they might consider changing.

- Help people create hypotheses related to, "If I did this," then "this might be the outcome."

- Reinforce the importance of stretching yourself a little beyond your comfort zone.

- Foster evaluation of the results after each experiment, testing multiple interpretations of each experiment and using the results to decide what the next experiment might be.

Materials

- Flip chart and markers

- Participant Handbook, Experiment Log

Time

- 30–45 minutes

Content Notes

It is important to reinforce that KLC understands the risk involved in exercising leadership and that no one should experiment with changing behavior without a clear purpose for doing so. You can also use the pushing beyond your comfort zone diagram (Figure 23), page 220. Depending on the type of KLC program, you can refer to previous mentions during the program of the idea of being experimental. These opportunities might have emerged during Case-in-Point, or Manage Self discussions.

Instructions

1. Name the competencies and principles that are related to designing experiments and being experimental (Manage Self and Intervene Skillfully).

2. Refer to the diagram of pushing beyond the comfort zone.

3. Reference and encourage thinking creatively through the formulation of some hypotheses. "If I did this" then "this might happen (to make progress toward my purpose)." Give several examples.

4. If you are using the participant handbook, the Experiment Log is the main focus. Ask learners to think of all the possible experiments they could undertake without beginning to judge what they would actually do or evaluating whether the experiments would be too risky. The goal is to list as many experiments as possible to consider at some point. If they have been through a 360°, they can easily link the "purpose of the experiments" to any

of the competencies or subpoints that stood out on their 360° self-assessment reports.

5. Once the learners have five or six experiments listed, walk them through the evaluation question list in the participant handbook and on Page 244 of this book.

6. The learners can then work in pairs or triads. They should test and challenge each other to see if they are pushing themselves outside their comfort zones and if their experiments should be considered a smart risk.

7. Move to the dashboard pages at the back of the participant handbook. Allow the learners to begin recording today's date and the status of their leadership challenge. Explain that they should set a date in the future when they will once again evaluate the challenge to see if they are making any progress. New experiments will most likely arise after each evaluation date.

CHAPTER 5

Raising the Bar

Raising the Bar

We live in a world where the complexity of dilemmas, scope of opportunities and range of choices cry out for more people willing and able to mobilize others to do difficult work.

Scan the headlines of any news website — be it local, national or global — and it becomes abundantly clear that we cannot count on those with high levels of authority to make our problems go away. In story after story, we see people in supposedly powerful positions grappling with the same difficult problems over and over again, with little progress to show for it.

KLC's principles and competencies are the distillation of what people told us about the kind of leadership it will take to bridge the gap between our current reality and our aspirations for healthy communities, prosperous companies and great institutions that meet the needs of people in all corners of the world. These are high-minded goals, and they require us to raise our level of aspiration for teaching leadership.

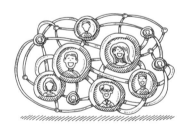

THE TEACHING METHODS YOU HAVE READ ABOUT HERE ARE CHALLENGING AND EXPERIENTIAL.

They shift the focus of teaching and coaching from maximizing individual power and influence to building the capacity of many people to mobilize others to do difficult work.

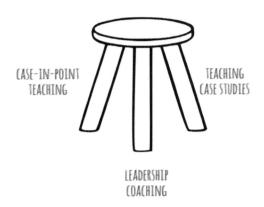

CASE-IN-POINT
TEACHING

TEACHING
CASE STUDIES

LEADERSHIP
COACHING

Our three-legged stool will always remain a work in progress as we continue to refine our approach and improve our results. We recognize that we are students of leadership and leadership development, constantly learning from colleagues and through our own experience. But the premise behind our three-legged stool is sound. Getting results with leadership training requires application of a progression of methods that together provide opportunities for realistic intensity (Case-in-Point), the application of theory to real-life situations (Case Teaching) and personalized support (Leadership Coaching). These methods prepare learners from all walks of life to contribute to a better world through leadership.

We encourage you to learn these methods and incorporate our three-legged stool approach. Over time, you will begin to experiment and tailor them to your own context. When you do, we hope you will share what you learn and develop with us.

Leadership brings with it a tension between holding to your purpose and meeting others where they are, a tension that can be lessened with

COMPASSION, INTENTION AND CREATIVITY.

We hope this book is a good resource and solid foundation upon which to begin practicing our methods and to unleash your imagination to use them in a way that most benefits those who learn from you and with you.

240

KLC is standing by to help you hone the skills and presence you need to create lasting change for the common good. If you found these methods intriguing, please sign up for our *Teaching Leadership* workshops or conferences to get instruction, practice and feedback on delivering the sessions. However you define excellence and wherever you are on your journey toward mastery, we are eager to travel with you.

Your role as a teacher brings with it a level of responsibility that we encourage you to consider. Those who learn with you will do much to shape our communities and the world through their work in business, government, faith communities, education and other parts of the nonprofit sector, as well as in the crucial spaces where sectors overlap and people come together to address shared issues.

Ultimately, your impact, and the value of our field overall, will be judged by

HOW WELL WE PREPARE LEARNERS TO MAKE ACTUAL PROGRESS.

If you take but one thing from this book, we hope it is the need to hold steadfast to that purpose, regardless of what competencies you teach or which methods you use. The stakes are high. Nothing less than the future is on the line.

Experiment Log

If teaching leadership is an adaptive challenge, then it makes sense that you will want to practice the four competencies and act experimentally as you apply the ideas contained in this book.

Thoughts about how to develop yourself will come to you as you read this book and practice teaching using these methods. Use the following pages to list these ideas — we'll call them experiments — as they occur to you. Think about the purpose of each experiment. Briefly describe what you'll do and when you'll do it. Take time to assess the risk, effort and probability of success for yourself and your learners.

Remember, the purpose behind experiments is to discover new things, to learn and grow in your role as a teacher, coach, facilitator or consultant. There is no such thing as failure as long as you maintain a "what did I learn?" mindset.

POSSIBLE EXPERIMENT

Purpose of the experiment:

What would you actually do?

Purpose of the experiment:

What would you actually do?

Purpose of the experiment:

What would you actually do?

Purpose of the experiment:

What would you actually do?

Purpose of the experiment:

What would you actually do?

Purpose of the experiment:

What would you actually do?

How much of a stretch is this for me?	How risky is this for me?	How sure am I that I will learn something?	How much effort will it take?
Big Stretch 7 6 5 4 3 2 1 No Stretch	High Risk 7 6 5 4 3 2 1 No Risk	Absolutely Sure 7 6 5 4 3 2 1 Not at all Sure	High Effort 7 6 5 4 3 2 1 No Effort
Big Stretch 7 6 5 4 3 2 1 No Stretch	High Risk 7 6 5 4 3 2 1 No Risk	Absolutely Sure 7 6 5 4 3 2 1 Not at all Sure	High Effort 7 6 5 4 3 2 1 No Effort
Big Stretch 7 6 5 4 3 2 1 No Stretch	High Risk 7 6 5 4 3 2 1 No Risk	Absolutely Sure 7 6 5 4 3 2 1 Not at all Sure	High Effort 7 6 5 4 3 2 1 No Effort
Big Stretch 7 6 5 4 3 2 1 No Stretch	High Risk 7 6 5 4 3 2 1 No Risk	Absolutely Sure 7 6 5 4 3 2 1 Not at all Sure	High Effort 7 6 5 4 3 2 1 No Effort
Big Stretch 7 6 5 4 3 2 1 No Stretch	High Risk 7 6 5 4 3 2 1 No Risk	Absolutely Sure 7 6 5 4 3 2 1 Not at all Sure	High Effort 7 6 5 4 3 2 1 No Effort
Big Stretch 7 6 5 4 3 2 1 No Stretch	High Risk 7 6 5 4 3 2 1 No Risk	Absolutely Sure 7 6 5 4 3 2 1 Not at all Sure	High Effort 7 6 5 4 3 2 1 No Effort

245

POSSIBLE EXPERIMENT

Purpose of the experiment:

What would you actually do?

Purpose of the experiment:

What would you actually do?

Purpose of the experiment:

What would you actually do?

Purpose of the experiment:

What would you actually do?

Purpose of the experiment:

What would you actually do?

Purpose of the experiment:

What would you actually do?

How much of a stretch is this for me?	How risky is this for me?	How sure am I that I will learn something?	How much effort will it take?
Big Stretch 7 6 5 4 3 2 1 No Stretch	High Risk 7 6 5 4 3 2 1 No Risk	Absolutely Sure 7 6 5 4 3 2 1 Not at all Sure	High Effort 7 6 5 4 3 2 1 No Effort
Big Stretch 7 6 5 4 3 2 1 No Stretch	High Risk 7 6 5 4 3 2 1 No Risk	Absolutely Sure 7 6 5 4 3 2 1 Not at all Sure	High Effort 7 6 5 4 3 2 1 No Effort
Big Stretch 7 6 5 4 3 2 1 No Stretch	High Risk 7 6 5 4 3 2 1 No Risk	Absolutely Sure 7 6 5 4 3 2 1 Not at all Sure	High Effort 7 6 5 4 3 2 1 No Effort
Big Stretch 7 6 5 4 3 2 1 No Stretch	High Risk 7 6 5 4 3 2 1 No Risk	Absolutely Sure 7 6 5 4 3 2 1 Not at all Sure	High Effort 7 6 5 4 3 2 1 No Effort
Big Stretch 7 6 5 4 3 2 1 No Stretch	High Risk 7 6 5 4 3 2 1 No Risk	Absolutely Sure 7 6 5 4 3 2 1 Not at all Sure	High Effort 7 6 5 4 3 2 1 No Effort
Big Stretch 7 6 5 4 3 2 1 No Stretch	High Risk 7 6 5 4 3 2 1 No Risk	Absolutely Sure 7 6 5 4 3 2 1 Not at all Sure	High Effort 7 6 5 4 3 2 1 No Effort

POSSIBLE EXPERIMENT

Purpose of the experiment:

What would you actually do?

Purpose of the experiment:

What would you actually do?

Purpose of the experiment:

What would you actually do?

Purpose of the experiment:

What would you actually do?

Purpose of the experiment:

What would you actually do?

Purpose of the experiment:

What would you actually do?

How much of a stretch is this for me?	How risky is this for me?	How sure am I that I will learn something?	How much effort will it take?
Big Stretch 7 6 5 4 3 2 1 No Stretch	High Risk 7 6 5 4 3 2 1 No Risk	Absolutely Sure 7 6 5 4 3 2 1 Not at all Sure	High Effort 7 6 5 4 3 2 1 No Effort
Big Stretch 7 6 5 4 3 2 1 No Stretch	High Risk 7 6 5 4 3 2 1 No Risk	Absolutely Sure 7 6 5 4 3 2 1 Not at all Sure	High Effort 7 6 5 4 3 2 1 No Effort
Big Stretch 7 6 5 4 3 2 1 No Stretch	High Risk 7 6 5 4 3 2 1 No Risk	Absolutely Sure 7 6 5 4 3 2 1 Not at all Sure	High Effort 7 6 5 4 3 2 1 No Effort
Big Stretch 7 6 5 4 3 2 1 No Stretch	High Risk 7 6 5 4 3 2 1 No Risk	Absolutely Sure 7 6 5 4 3 2 1 Not at all Sure	High Effort 7 6 5 4 3 2 1 No Effort
Big Stretch 7 6 5 4 3 2 1 No Stretch	High Risk 7 6 5 4 3 2 1 No Risk	Absolutely Sure 7 6 5 4 3 2 1 Not at all Sure	High Effort 7 6 5 4 3 2 1 No Effort
Big Stretch 7 6 5 4 3 2 1 No Stretch	High Risk 7 6 5 4 3 2 1 No Risk	Absolutely Sure 7 6 5 4 3 2 1 Not at all Sure	High Effort 7 6 5 4 3 2 1 No Effort

Notes

Notes

Notes

Notes

Notes

Notes

Notes

Notes

Notes

Notes

Notes

Notes

Works Consulted

Introduction

Erhard, Werner, Jensen, Michael, and Granger, Kari. (2012). Creating Leaders: An Ontological/Phenomenological Model. In Snook, Scott, Nohria, Nitin, & Khurana, Rakesh (Eds.), *The Handbook for Teaching Leadership: Knowing, Doing, Being.* (245-264). Thousand Oaks, CA: Sage Publications.

Kellerman, Barbara. *Leadership: Essential Selections on Power, Authority, and Influence.* 2010.

Mesirow, Jack. *Learning as Transformation.* San Francisco, CA: John Wiley & Sons, 2000.

Chapter 1: Case-in-Point

Rogers, Jenny. *Adults Learning.* Berkshire, England: McGraw-Hill Education, 2007.

Heifetz, Ronald and Linsky, Marty. *Leadership on the Line: Staying Alive Through the Dangers of Leading,* Cambridge, MA: Harvard Business School Press, 2002.

Heifetz, Ronald. *Leadership Without Easy Answers.* Cambridge, MA: Harvard University Press, 1994.

Johnstone, Michael and Fern, Maxime. "CIP: An Experiential Methodology for Leadership Education," *The Journal of Kansas Civic Leadership Development,* Vol. 2, Issue 2, Fall 2010.

Parks, Sharon Daloz. *Leadership Can Be Taught.* Boston, MA: Harvard Business School Press, 2005.

Chapter 2: Teaching Case Studies

Barnes, Louis B., et. al. "Teaching and the Case Method," Text, Cases and Readings, 3rd Edition. Cambridge, MA: Harvard Business School Press, 1994.

Boehrer, John. "How to Teach a Case," Harvard University, John F. Kennedy School of Government Case Program, Case No. C18-95-1285.0, 1995.

Christiansen Center for Teaching and Learning, www.hbs.edu/teaching/inside-hbs/, March 2015

Gomez-Ibanez, Jose A. "Learning by the Case Method," Harvard University, John F. Kennedy School of Government Case Program, Case No. N15-86-1136.0, 1986.

Gragg, Charles I. "Because Wisdom Can't Be Told," Harvard Business School, Case No. 9-451-005, Rev. November 30, 1982.

Hammond, John S. "Learning by the Case Method," Harvard Business School, Case No. 9-376-241, Rev. April 16, 2002.

Heifetz, Ronald A., Linsky, Marty, and Grashow, Alexander. "The Practice of Adaptive Leadership: Tools and Tactics for Changing Your Organization and the World," Harvard Business Press, 2009.

Husock, Howard. "Using a Teaching Case," Harvard University, John F. Kennedy School of Government Case Program, 2000.

O'Malley, Ed. "The Competencies for Civic Leadership: An Introduction to the Curricular Underpinnings of the KLC," The Journal of Kansas Civic Leadership Development, Vol. 1, Issue 1, Spring 2009.

Robyn, Dorothy. "What Makes a Good Case," Harvard University, John F. Kennedy School of Government Case Program, Case No. N15-86-673.0, 1986.

Winston, Kenneth I. "Teaching Ethics by the Case Method," Harvard University, John F. Kennedy School of Government Case Program, Case No. N18-95-1304.0, 1995.

Chapter 3: Coaching to Make Progress on Adaptive Challenges

Coachville.com. *The Coaching Starter Kit: Everything You Need to Launch and Expand Your Coaching Practice.* New York, NY: Norton, 2003.

Flaherty, James. *Coaching: Evoking Excellence in Others, 3rd edition.* Burlington, MA: Elsevier, 2011.

International Coach Federation. *Individual Credentialing and Core Competencies.* http://www.coachfederation.org/getcredentialed/. March 2015.

Kegan, Robert and Lahey, Lisa Laskow. *Immunity to Change Immunity to Change: How to Overcome It and Unlock the Potential in Yourself and Your Organization.* Boston, MA: Harvard Business School Publishing, 2009.

Lasley, Martha, Kellogg, Virginia, Michaels, Richard, and Brown, Sharon. *Coaching for Transformation: Pathways to Ignite Personal and Social Change.* Troy, PA: Discover Press, 2011.

Maruska, Don and Perry, Jay. Foreword by Kouzas, Jim. *Take Charge of Your Talent: Three Keys to Thriving in Your Career Organization and Life.* San Francisco, CA: Berrett-Koehler, 2013.

McNamara, Carter. *Authenticity Circles Facilitator's Guide: A Step-by-Step Guide to Facilitating Peer Coaching Groups.* Minneapolis, MN: Authenticity Consulting, 2002.

O'Neill, Mary Beth A. *Executive Coaching with Backbone and Heart: A Systems Approach to Engaging Leaders with Their Challenges.* San Francisco, CA: Jossey-Bass, 2007.

Rogers, Jenny. *Coaching Skills: A Handbook, 3rd edition.* Maidenhead, Berkshire, England: Open University Press, 2012.

Rosinski, Philippe. *Global Coaching: An Integrated Approach for Long-Last Results.* Boston, MA: Brealey, 2010.

Stoltzfus, Tony. *Coaching Questions: A Coach's Guide to Powerful Asking Skills*. Virginia Beach, VA: Coach22.com, 2008.

Silsbee, Doug. *Presence-Based Coaching: Cultivating Self-Generative Leaders Through Mind, Body, and Heart*. San Francisco, CA: Jossey-Bass, 2008.

Whitworth, Laura, Kimsey-House, Karen, Kimsey-House, Henry, and Sandahl, Phillip. *Co-Active Coaching, 2nd Edition: New Skills for Coaching People Toward Success in Work and, Life* (Paperback - Feb 25, 2007).

Williams, Patrick, and Menendez, Diane S. *Becoming a Professional Life Coach: Lessons for the Institute for Life Coach Training*. New York, NY: Norton, 2007.

Williams, Patrick, and Thomas, Lloyd J. *Total Life Coaching: 50+ Life Lessons, Skills, and Techniques to Enhance Your Practice … and Your Life*. New York, NY: Norton, 2005.

Wilson, Judith, Gislason, Michelle, and CompassPoint Nonprofit Services. *Coaching Skills for Nonprofit Managers and Leaders: Developing People to Achieve Your Mission*. San Francisco, CA: Jossey-Bass, 2010.

Acknowledgments

Countless KLC staff, faculty, coaches, consultants and program participants have contributed to the development of the ideas contained in this book. Ron Alexander, Kevin Bomhoff, David Chrislip, Peter Cohen, Jan Davis, Matt Jordan, Lynette Lacy, Tim Link, Ed O'Malley and Tim Steffensmeier deserve special thanks.

Marty Linsky, Ron Heifetz, Jeff Lawrence and Cambridge Leadership Associates have been key partners since 2007, especially helping us explore the nature of adaptive challenges and the use of Case-in-Point teaching.

For feedback during the editing process we thank Laura Goodman, Paula Haas, Sarah Caldwell Hancock, Shannon Littlejohn, Mike Matson, Diana Renner and Mary Tolar.

For creative direction and project management we thank Amy Nichols.

We are thankful to the members of the Kansas Leadership Center board of directors, robust and critical thought partners whose commitment to the mission drives everything we do.

Finally, we are grateful for the visionary leadership of the Kansas Health Foundation, which in 2006 decided a statewide center to develop civic leadership was and forever would be essential.

About the Authors

Chris Green is the managing editor of The Journal, KLC's quarterly magazine created to inspire leadership for the common good. He began working with the Kansas Leadership Center in 2009.

Julia Fabris McBride is the vice president of the Kansas Leadership Center and has a background in theater and executive coaching. She joined the Kansas Leadership Center in 2008.

Kansas Leadership Center Leadership Principles and Competencies

Leadership Principles

1. Leadership is an activity, not a position.

2. Anyone can lead, anytime, anywhere.

3. It starts with you and must engage others.

4. Your purpose must be clear.

5. It's risky.

Four Competencies of Leadership

Diagnose Situation

- Explore tough interpretations
- Distinguish technical and adaptive work
- Understand the process challenges
- Test multiple interpretations and points of view
- Take the temperature
- Identify who needs to do the work

Energize Others

- Engage unusual voices
- Work across factions
- Start where they are
- Speak to loss
- Inspire a collective purpose
- Create a trustworthy process

Manage Self

- Know your strengths, vulnerabilities and triggers
- Know the story others tell about you
- Choose among competing values
- Get used to uncertainty and conflict
- Experiment beyond your comfort zone
- Take care of yourself

Intervene Skillfully

- Make conscious choices
- Raise the heat
- Give the work back
- Hold to purpose
- Speak from the heart
- Act experimentally

Teaching Leadership

Help people create the life they want, the change they desire and the culture they imagine. Join a community of practice to increase your capacity to help more people make progress.

KLC offers *Teaching Leadership* conferences and workshops for teachers, coaches, facilitators, consultants, mentors and leadership program directors. A wide range of workshops allow participants to hone in on specific knowledge and individual skill sets related to the art of teaching, coaching and facilitation.

Register at:
www.kansasleadershipcenter.org/teachingleadership

About the Kansas Leadership Center

The Kansas Leadership Center was established by the Kansas Health Foundation to add significant value to the leadership development efforts undertaken by the foundation since its early days.

With programs including *You.Lead.Now.* and *Lead for Change,* the Kansas Leadership Center equips people in community, business, faith, government and nonprofit sectors with skills to make positive change for the common good.

The Kansas Leadership Center is headquartered in downtown Wichita, Kansas.

325 E. Douglas Ave.
Wichita, KS 67202
www.kansasleadershipcenter.org
316.712.4950